FEED YOUR FAMILY FOR A FIV£R

IN UNDER **30** MINUTES

FEED YOUR FAMILY FOR A FIV£R

IN UNDER 30 MINUTES

MITCH LANE

Thorsons

WHEN USING KITCHEN APPLIANCES PLEASE ALWAYS
FOLLOW THE MANUFACTURER'S INSTRUCTIONS

Thorsons
An imprint of HarperCollins*Publishers*
1 London Bridge Street
London SE1 9GF

www.harpercollins.co.uk

HarperCollins*Publishers*
Macken House, 39/40 Mayor Street Upper
Dublin 1, D01 C9W8, Ireland

First published by Thorsons 2024

1 3 5 7 9 10 8 6 4 2

A catalogue record of this book is available from the British Library

ISBN 978-0-00-864951-7

Photographer: Tom Regester
Food Stylist: Katie Marshall
Prop Stylist: Max Robinson

Printed and bound by GPS Group in Bosnia-Herzegovina

This book contains FSC™ certified paper and other controlled
sources to ensure responsible forest management.

For more information visit: www.harpercollins.co.uk/green

Contents

Introduction

I'm Mitch, AKA @mealsbymitch. I'm from Wolverhampton and most of you will probably know me from TikTok and Instagram as either 'The Bon Appetit Guy' or 'That Brummie Fiver Meals Bloke'. In a nutshell, I show people how to cook on a tight budget! First of all, if you're reading this, you are now the proud owner of my new book *Feed Your Family for a Fiver in under 30 Minutes* and I want to say a massive thank you for buying it. It means so much to me and I just wanted to take the time to say that you are wonderful! To tell you the truth, I never thought I'd be sat here writing an introduction to a cookbook, let alone writing one for a second time! It's all quite surreal.

Just because it's cheap, it doesn't mean it has to taste cheap.

We all know how difficult it is these days with the cost of living taking its toll. Every time I go into the supermarket it seems the price of something has gone up. Everything is constantly on the rise and we're all having to dig deeper and deeper into our pockets to sustain even just a basic standard of living. Times really are tough. And on top of that there is hardly any time left after work, school runs, college, housework etc. So that's where this book comes in; I want all you busy and budget-conscious folk to still be able to enjoy an incredibly tasty and comforting meals without breaking the bank. And with a bit of careful planning, you can make all these recipes within half an hour too. Cheap and quick, it's what we all need these days! Oh, and just because it's cheap, it doesn't mean it has to taste cheap. It's all about creating big and bold flavours from very humble ingredients.

All these recipes have been stripped back to be as cost effective as possible for you. The ingredients are super accessible; you won't need to travel to the Himalayas to find a special type of truffle-infused oil! It's not fancy cooking, it's simple and wholesome family grub.

I've based each recipe on costing a fiver, so you should be able to walk into the supermarket with five quid and come out with change to make the entire meal. All I'm expecting you to have in your cupboards is salt and pepper and some cooking oil – everything else is included in the budget! The beauty of it is that most of the recipes are likely to cost even less. Top tip incoming: when you're writing your shopping list, try to pick recipes where there are crossover ingredients to save even more cash! You will find some recipes have an 'In the Basket' box. This gives a bit more information on how much of an ingredient I was able to buy for the budget and what you might have left over for another recipe.

The reality is that not all of us have got big, fancy and extravagant kitchens with state-of-the-art equipment. Don't worry if you're lacking in the cooking appliance department! I speak for myself when I say my kitchen is the size of a cupboard … I can almost touch it wall to wall! All these recipes are based on using the most basic of kitchen appliances. If you've got an oven, hob and a microwave then you're on for a winner.

I understand that cooking can be quite daunting for a lot of people; my best advice is to just have a go! We've all got to start somewhere and it really doesn't matter if you make a mistake or fail on your first attempt. I've designed these recipes to be as simple as possible for even the most inexperienced cook. Anybody of any skillset can have a crack at making these, I promise you! Just think of it in simple terms; all you are doing is putting some ingredients into a pan at the right time. Step out of your comfort zone and have a go! There's plenty to choose from. I've got all sorts in this book to cater for everyone ... pastas, one-pan meals, homemade curries, picky and buffet-style food, burgers, stuff to make with your leftovers and even a few little sweet treats, too.

I've designed these recipes to be as simple as possible for even the most inexperienced cook.

You just need to get into the budget meals mindset. We have to be real with ourselves and know from the get-go that we are not going to be able to afford branded items, expensive cuts of meat, free range and organic specially selected fresh ingredients. The reality is it's just not possible working on a tight budget unfortunately. If it's a choice between feeding my kids or buying free range, then I'm setting my moral compass aside and choosing to feed my kids. Here's a few of my tried-and-tested tips to get the most out of your budget and this book:

- As already mentioned, when planning your shopping list pick recipes that have crossover ingredients to save even more money. Choose a couple of recipes that both need soy sauce or curry powder, for example. It will help to consolidate the costs.

- Stock up on your traditional cupboard staples, such as salt, black pepper, vegetable oil, olive oil, plain flour and a range of stock cubes.

- Buy supermarket own-brand items, such as tinned tomatoes, pasta, seasonings and rice etc. Most of the time they're half the price (if not even cheaper) than branded items and taste just as good.

- When buying fresh ingredients, don't be afraid of using the 'wonky' or 'imperfect' ranges. Just because it doesn't look like your traditional onion or carrot, doesn't mean it's not going to taste like one! Once it's chopped up and cooked, you're never going to know the difference. Also, buy fresh stuff as singles. If you only need one pepper, then just buy one pepper. It's far cheaper to buy things loose as opposed to pre-packaged. If you have a local greengrocers, then take a look in there too, there are some right bargains to be found.

- Focus on getting the most for your money with the cheaper cuts of meat, such as chicken legs, 20% fat beef mince, cheap sausages and frozen fish fillets (as opposed to fresh). All these minor changes will make such a massive difference to your shopping bill, trust me. Plus, in my opinion chicken on the bone and the higher fat content beef taste better anyway!

- Make a plan of action before you do your food shop. Make a list of exactly what you need to get and stick to it.

- I've lost count of the number of times I've fallen guilty of this one, but try to go into the supermarket on a full stomach! Otherwise, you'll end up chucking in all that junk food when you go down the sweets and crisp aisles.

- If you don't have a lot of money, then please don't think for a second that you have to live on boring food, instant noodles or microwave meals. You can truly create some showstopper stuff without having to spend a fortune. I really do hope that you can find something in this book that you and your family love and I hope it can save you some hard-earned cash on your food bill too!

Perfect
Pasta

18

28

34

41

One-pan Lasagne

Family life is busy, so I don't have a lot of time on weekdays
to cook up a storm in the kitchen. This is a simple way
of making lasagne in half an hour that will definitely not
disappoint. I swap beef or pork mince for sausages because
they are cheaper and packed full of seasoning, so they give
the dish more of a punch. Enjoy!

Ingredients

8 pork sausages
2 tbsp olive oil
1 onion, finely chopped
3 garlic cloves, finely chopped
1 tbsp tomato purée
400g tin chopped tomatoes
300ml beef stock (made from
    a cube)
10 dried lasagne sheets
handful of fresh basil, finely
    chopped
125g ball mozzarella
salt and black pepper

🗑 IN THE BASKET

Tomato puree: based on a
200g tube

Lasagne sheets: based on a
500g packet

Garlic: based on a whole bulb

Stock cubes: based on a box of 8

Basil: based on a 30g packet

Method

1. Start by taking off the sausage skins. An easy way to do this is to
    take a sharp knife and carefully pierce the skin and slice down the
    length of the sausage. You should then be able to peel the skin away
    from the meat.

2. Break the sausages into small pieces with slightly damp hands
    (to stop the meat sticking to them) and then bash the meat with
    a wooden spoon or spatula to break it into even smaller pieces.
    Season with salt and pepper.

3. Put a frying pan on a high heat and add the olive oil. Cook the
    sausage meat until it starts to brown. It should only take about
    3–4 minutes to cook. When the meat is brown and starting to go
    crispy, take it out of the pan and set it aside.

4. Add the onion and let it cook for 2 minutes until it begins to soften,
    then add the garlic and cook for a further minute.

5. Return the sausage meat to the pan then add the tomato purée. Stir
    it through and cook for 1 minute. Add the tomatoes and beef stock
    and stir.

6. Add some more salt and pepper and let the mixture simmer on a
    low heat for 10 minutes while you put the lasagne sheets into some
    salted boiling water to soften.

7. When the lasagne sheets have softened, add them to the sauce and
    submerge them! The lasagne may look a complete mess, but it's
    going to taste great!

8. Add the basil and mix through. Break the mozzarella ball into chunks
    and spread them over the top.

9. Put the pan under a hot grill for 2–3 minutes to melt and colour the
    mozzarella.

10. Sprinkle more basil on top and serve.

Arrabbiata Penne

This is a simple, fresh and tasty pasta dish that you can throw together in 15 minutes. You can tweak the heat and up the quantity of chillies if you want it a little spicier. You can eat it hot or wait for it to cool down and have it the following day for lunch.

Ingredients

2 tbsp olive oil
1 red chilli, thinly sliced
4 garlic cloves, thinly sliced
330g cherry tomatoes, halved
300g penne
50g Parmesan, grated, plus extra
    to serve
handful of fresh basil, finely
    chopped
salt and black pepper

Method

1. Put a pan on a low heat and pour in the olive oil, then add the chilli and garlic. Let them soften for 1 minute.
2. Add the tomatoes with some salt and black pepper to taste. They will take about 5 minutes to soften and break down in the pan.
3. While the tomatoes are softening, put the penne into some salted boiling water. When it is al dente (still slightly firm), start to spoon it into the tomatoes along with half a ladle (about 50ml) of the pasta water.
4. Add the Parmesan and give everything a toss. The pasta water, cheese and tomatoes will begin to form a silky sauce.
5. Add the basil and toss again for 30 seconds before plating up and finishing with a crack of black pepper and a dusting of Parmesan.

IN THE BASKET

Chillies: based on a 65g packet

Garlic: based on a whole bulb

Pasta: based on a 500g packet

Basil: based on a 30g packet

Parmesan: based on a 100g block

Bacon and Pesto Gnocchi

Supper doesn't get much simpler than this: all you need are five ingredients and I'm including black pepper in that. This is a great tasting dish using minimal effort – your midweek meal can be ready in 15 minutes! If you're not a fan of green food, then look away now …

Ingredients

300g bacon, cut into 2cm pieces
500g gnocchi
190g jar green or basil pesto
50g Grana Padano, grated, plus extra to serve
black pepper

Method

1. Put the bacon pieces into a cold frying pan and gradually increase the heat to render the fat and ensure that the bacon ends up nice and crispy.
2. As soon as the bacon starts to darken in colour, bring a pan of salted water to the boil and put the gnocchi into it. When the gnocchi float to the top of the water, they're done and ready to eat. Drain, reserving some of the cooking water.
3. Add the gnocchi to the crispy bacon along with the entire jar of pesto, the Grana Padano and half a ladle (about 50ml) of the cooking water.
4. Toss everything together in the frying pan for 30 seconds, then plate up and add a crack of black pepper on top, along with another dusting of Parmesan to finish.

IN THE BASKET

Grana Padano: based on a 100g packet

Deconstructed Cheeseburger Pasta

This sounds so wrong, but tastes so right. I've taken a classic cheeseburger and turned it into a pasta dish! Looks like pasta, but tastes exactly like a cheeseburger. You can even make the cheese sauce by using burger cheese squares. It's a winner in my house, and I know it will be a winner in yours too! Unless you don't like burgers of course ... but who doesn't enjoy a good burger?

Ingredients

½ tbsp vegetable oil

500g 20% fat minced beef

½ onion, finely diced

400g penne

15 burger cheese slices or cheesy singles, broken into 2cm pieces

50ml milk

3–4 pickled gherkins or jalapeños, finely diced, plus 2 tbsp of the pickle juice

sauce to finish (I use American-style mustard and ketchup)

salt and black pepper

Method

1. Put a pan over a high heat and add the oil and beef. Break the mince into small pieces – you don't want any big clumps. You can use the back of a wooden spoon or even a whisk. Season the meat generously with salt and black pepper. Try to avoid moving it around the pan too much; you want a nice brown crust to replicate the traditional smash burger sear.

2. When the meat starts to form a brown crust, add the onion and continue to cook for 2–3 minutes until the meat is cooked through and onion has softened.

3. Meanwhile, bring a pan of salted water to the boil and add the penne to it.

4. Take the meat and onion out of the pan and drain off any excess fat using a sieve or colander. Wipe the pan clean and put it back over a low heat.

5. Put the cheese squares in the pan along with the milk and continuously stir the mixture over a low heat until it begins to form an orange cheesy sauce. Season with salt and pepper.

6. When the penne is cooked, spoon it into the cheesy sauce and then add the minced beef. Mix everything together.

7. Top with the finely diced gherkins and the pickle juice and finally your chosen burger sauce.

IN THE BASKET

Pasta: based on a 500g packet

Milk: based on a 1 pint bottle

Gherkins: based on a 340g jar

Cheesy Broccoli Gnocchi

If you're a big fan of cheese, you'll be in heaven with this. Creamy, cheesy, indulgent and incredibly comforting. I'm drooling just thinking about it. For speed, I stick this under the grill to melt the cheese (as opposed to oven baking). I don't want to wait ages for a meal on a midweek evening. To put it simply, I'm mixing some ingredients in a pan, transferring them to a baking dish, topping them with cheese and grilling them. Nice and easy!

Ingredients

3 tbsp olive oil
500g gnocchi
1 head broccoli, florets cut into
   3cm chunks, stalk peeled and
   finely chopped
1 tsp chilli flakes
2 tsp garlic granules
200g soft cheese or cream cheese
125g ball mozzarella
salt and black pepper

Method

1. Heat the grill to high.
2. Meanwhile, put a pan over a high heat and add the oil. Add the gnocchi, broccoli florets and stalk, chilli flakes, garlic granules and a generous pinch of salt and black pepper. Give everything a good toss together in the pan and cook for 3–4 minutes until the gnocchi begins to go golden.
3. Add the soft cheese and stir it through for 1 minute.
4. Transfer everything to a baking dish, break up the ball of mozzarella and spread it over the top. Put the dish of gnocchi under the grill for 4–5 minutes until the cheese melts and turns beautifully golden.

IN THE BASKET

Chilli flakes: based on a 29g jar

Garlic granules: based on a 52g jar

Bacon and Leek Spaghetti

This is an incredibly quick and easy pasta dish. You only need to buy five ingredients – and believe me, this one is a people pleaser. Really comforting and a meal to look forward to.

Ingredients

8 slices smoked bacon, cut into 2cm pieces
300g spaghetti
1 leek, cut into 2cm chunks
2 garlic cloves, finely chopped
100g Parmesan or Pecorino Romano, plus extra to serve
salt and black pepper

Method

1. Put the bacon pieces into a dry cold frying pan and gradually heat until it is hot. This helps to render the fat. Cook the bacon until it begins to go crispy – about 3–4 minutes.
2. Bring a large pan of salted water to the boil and cook the spaghetti according to the packet instructions until it is al dente (still slightly firm). The spaghetti will cook a bit more in the pan with the bacon so it shouldn't be too soggy at this point. Drain, reserving some of the pasta water.
3. While the spaghetti cooks, add the leek and garlic to the bacon pan, turn down the heat to low and cook them gently.
4. Start mixing spaghetti strands into the bacon and leek mixture, along with a generous ladle of pasta water.
5. Add the cheese and mix everything together thoroughly. The pasta water and cheese will combine to create a sauce. Add a little more pasta water if you want a looser sauce, or more cheese to make it thicker. Make sure the spaghetti strands don't stick together – you want the dish to be light and silky.
6. Plate up and finish with a few cracks of black pepper and a dusting of cheese.

IN THE BASKET

Spaghetti: based on a 500g packet

Garlic: based on a whole bulb

Parmesan: based on a 200g block

Garlic granules: based on a 52g jar

Chilli Con Carne Macaroni

This is so simple, yet just so tasty. I love a good chilli con carne as much as the next guy but have you ever combined it with macaroni to make an amazing pasta dish? It's an unlikely combination but it's the real deal! If you want to tweak it slightly you could add a pepper or some jalapeños or even increase the heat by adding more chillies.

Ingredients

2 tbsp olive oil
1 onion, finely diced
1 red chilli, finely diced, plus thin
   slices to serve
4 garlic cloves, minced
500g 20% fat minced beef
41g packet chilli con carne
   seasoning mix (see page 62 for
   how to make your own)
400g tin chopped tomatoes
215g tin kidney beans, drained
300g macaroni
125g mozzarella ball
handful of coriander, finely
   chopped (optional)
salt and black pepper

Method

1. Put a pan on a medium heat and add the olive oil, onion and chilli. Let them cook and soften for 2 minutes. Add the garlic and continue to cook for 1 minute.
2. Add the beef and break it up with the back of a wooden spoon in the pan, ensuring that there are no big clumps. Brown the meat for 3–4 minutes.
3. Tip in the seasoning mix and add salt and pepper to taste, then stir the contents of the pan and cook for another minute.
4. Pour in the tomatoes, beans and 100ml of tap water. Let this sauce simmer and bubble away on a low heat while you cook the macaroni.
5. Bring a pan of salted water to the boil and put in the macaroni. Cook until tender, then drain.
6. Spoon the cooked macaroni into the chilli con carne mixture. Break up the ball of mozzarella and stir it through to make the mixture nice and cheesy.
7. Add a handful of coriander (if using) and sprinkle some thin chilli slices over the top to serve.

IN THE BASKET

Chillies: based on a 65g packet
Garlic: based on a whole bulb
Pasta: based on a 500g packet

Pizza Pasta

You should know by now that I've got you covered when it comes to making a quick, cheap and easy pasta dish. This recipe combines ingredients from two of my favourite meals – pizza and pasta! If you can't decide which you want, then combine the two to make this tasty, family-pleasing meal! This is super versatile and you can use your favourite pizza toppings, such as peppers, sweetcorn, jalapeños and so on. This recipe is pepperoni pizza-style but feel free to tweak it to your taste and preferences. There are some mouthwatering cheese pulls in this one – enjoy!

Ingredients

1 tbsp olive oil
70g pack sliced pepperoni
½ red onion, finely chopped
4 garlic cloves, finely chopped
2 x 400g tins chopped tomatoes
handful of fresh basil, finely
   chopped, plus extra to serve
400g rigatoni
2 x 125g balls mozzarella
salt and black pepper

Method

1. Put a pan on a medium heat and add the olive oil, then half the pepperoni slices and the onion. Cook for 2 minutes until the onion begins to soften. Add the garlic and cook for a further minute.

2. Add the tomatoes and salt and pepper to taste. Stir through the basil and let the sauce bubble away for 10 minutes.

3. Meanwhile, bring a pan of salted water to the boil and cook the rigatoni according to the packet instructions, then drain.

4. Spoon the pasta into the sauce and mix it through, ensuring that all the pasta is generously coated in the sauce.

5. Break up one of the mozzarella balls and mix it through the sauce to make it nice and cheesy. Turn off the heat at this point and break up the second mozzarella ball and spread it over the top of the pasta.

6. Scatter the rest of the pepperoni over the top of the pasta.

7. Heat the grill to high and put the pan underneath to melt the cheese and crisp up the pepperoni.

8. Serve with some more basil.

IN THE BASKET

Garlic: based on a whole bulb

Basil: based on a 30g packet

Pasta: based on a 500g packet

Speedy Veggie Pasta 'Bake'

Now this is a pasta bake that you don't actually bake! I want supper to be quick. I don't want to wait for it to spend half an hour in the oven, I want it to be ready in a total of 15 minutes! This is a great little recipe that you can chuck together in no time at all after work.

Ingredients

1 tbsp olive oil
1 red onion, chopped into
    2cm chunks
1 red pepper, chopped into
    2cm chunks
1 green pepper, chopped into
    2cm chunks
1 courgette, chopped into
    2cm chunks
1 carrot, chopped into 2cm chunks
mixed herbs or chilli flakes
    (optional)
4 garlic cloves, minced
2 x 400g tins chopped tomatoes
400g pasta (I use conchiglie)
125g ball mozzarella
salt and black pepper

Method

1. Put a pan on a high heat and add the olive oil, onion, peppers, courgette and carrot. Season generously with salt and pepper and add the mixed herbs or chilli flakes (if using) at this stage.
2. Cook the vegetables for 2 minutes and then add the garlic. Let it cook for a further minute.
3. Add the tomatoes, turn the heat down to low and let the mixture simmer while you cook the pasta.
4. Bring a pan of salted water to the boil and cook the pasta according to the packet instructions. Drain and then spoon the pasta into the pan of vegetables.
5. Give everything a good stir and then break up the ball of mozzarella and spread it over the top.
6. Heat the grill to high and put the pan under for 2 minutes until the cheese has melted.

IN THE BASKET

Garlic: based on a whole bulb

Pasta: based on a 500g packet

Mushroom, Spinach and Ricotta Tagliatelle

Here's another wonderfully simple pasta dish! You just need five ingredients (plus oil and salt and pepper) to make an elegant-tasting dish. You can throw this one together in just over the time it takes the pasta to soften. Ingredients needed: five, brain cells needed: zero. Easy, economical and incredibly fresh tasting using very basic ingredients.

Ingredients

400g tagliatelle
2 tbsp olive oil
300g closed cup mushrooms, quartered
6 garlic cloves, minced
150g fresh spinach
250g tub ricotta
salt and black pepper

Method

1. Bring a pan of salted water to the boil and put in the tagliatelle. Cook according to the packet instructions then drain, reserving some of the cooking water.
2. Put another pan over a medium heat and add the oil and mushrooms. Let them cook for 2 minutes. Add the minced garlic and cook for a further minute.
3. Add the spinach and let it wilt for 30 seconds, then tip in the ricotta along with a ladle (about 50ml) of the pasta water and mix everything together. If you want the sauce to be a little more liquid, add more pasta water.
4. Add the cooked tagliatelle and mix everything together. If you're feeling adventurous, try tossing the contents of the pan.
5. Season to taste with salt and pepper and serve.

🧺 IN THE BASKET

Tagliatelle: based on a 500g packet

Garlic: based on a whole bulb

Spinach: based on a 240g packet

Sausage Gnocchi

This is a simple six-ingredient recipe that you can put together in 20 minutes. To save as much time as possible, I use ready-made gnocchi. When it comes to a midweek meal, I don't want to cook anything time consuming. I remember the first time I made this I used the food I had in my cupboards and fridge so the recipe came together as a bit of an accident. But it tastes so good and it's properly comforting.

Ingredients

1 tbsp olive oil
8 pork sausages (or any sausage of
    your choice)
½ onion, finely chopped
2 garlic cloves, finely chopped
400g tin chopped tomatoes
500g gnocchi
50g Parmesan or Pecorino
    Romano, grated, plus extra
    to serve
salt and black pepper

Method

1. Put a pan on a high heat and add the olive oil. Remove the sausages from their skins by carefully piercing the skin and slicing down the length of each sausage. You should be able to peel the skin away from the meat. Break up the sausage meat into small chunks and put them into the pan. If you run your hands under cold water it helps to prevent the meat from sticking to your hands.
2. Break up the sausage meat with the back of a wooden spoon into smaller pieces and cook for 4–5 minutes until they are golden brown and semi-crispy. Take them out of the pan and set them aside.
3. Lower the heat under the pan to medium and add the onion along with a pinch of salt. Cook for 3 minutes until it begins to soften. Add the garlic and cook for a further minute.
4. Tip in the tomatoes and return the sausage meat to the pan, give everything a stir and turn the heat down to low.
5. Bring a pan of salted water to the boil and cook the gnocchi. They will only take about 2 minutes to soften. As soon as they begin to float in the water, they are ready to eat.
6. Spoon the gnocchi into the sausage and tomato pan along with a generous ladle (about 50ml) of cooking water.
7. Add the Parmesan and toss everything together. If you want a more liquid sauce then add a little more water.
8. Plate up and add a crack of black pepper along with another dusting of grated Parmesan.

IN THE BASKET

Garlic: based on a whole bulb

Parmesan: based on a 100g block

Roasted Red Pepper and Tomato Penne

I absolutely love pasta recipes that can be completed in the time it takes the pasta to cook. This is a great example of one of those. Simply put the pasta on to boil, chuck a load of ingredients into a food processor, blitz them and then bring everything together in a pan. It's so easy that I reckon even my five-year-old could make it. I use jarred chargrilled peppers for quickness and this is a great way of adding instant flavour.

Ingredients

350g penne
400g tin tomatoes
170g jar chargrilled peppers
50g Parmesan, grated, plus extra
   to serve
3 garlic cloves
10 basil leaves, plus extra to serve
2 tbsp olive oil
salt and black pepper

Method

1. Bring a pan of salted water to the boil and add the pasta. Cook according to the packet instructions then drain.
2. Put the tomatoes, peppers, Parmesan, garlic, basil, oil and a couple of cracks of black pepper into a food processor. Blitz until smooth.
3. Put a pan over a low heat and add the blitzed mixture. Bring it up to a simmer.
4. Spoon the pasta into the sauce and mix everything together.
5. Plate up, add another crack of black pepper, a sprinkling of Parmesan and some basil to finish.

IN THE BASKET

Pasta: based on a 500g packet

Parmesan: based on a 100g block

Garlic: based on a whole bulb

Basil: based on a 30g packet

Hidden Veggie Pasta

This is the ultimate pasta recipe for getting as many vegetables into your kids as possible without them knowing! My kids don't like peppers or courgettes, but they demolish this meal whenever I cook it. It works like magic. That's not to say that adults won't like it though – I absolutely love it too! You can experiment with swapping the veggies you put in, but this combination works every single time. Oh, and just to mention – it's cheap, quick and easy too.

Ingredients

1 tbsp vegetable or olive oil
1 onion, finely chopped
2 carrots, finely chopped
1 courgette, finely chopped
1 red pepper, finely chopped
1 stick celery, finely chopped
4 garlic cloves, finely chopped
400g tin tomatoes
500ml vegetable stock (made
   from a cube)
300g pasta
salt and black pepper

Method

1. Put a pan on a medium heat and add the oil, onion, carrots, courgette, pepper and celery along with a pinch of salt. Let the vegetables soften and cook for 4–5 minutes.
2. Add the garlic and continue to cook for 1 minute. Add the tomatoes and vegetable stock and let the mixture bubble away while you cook the pasta.
3. Bring a pan of salted water to the boil, add the pasta and cook according to the packet instructions, then drain.
4. Use a hand blender or food processor to blend the sauce until it is smooth.
5. Spoon the cooked pasta into the sauce and stir it through.
6. Taste and season with salt and black pepper.

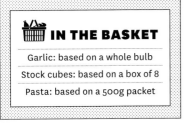

IN THE BASKET

Garlic: based on a whole bulb

Stock cubes: based on a box of 8

Pasta: based on a 500g packet

Jerk Pasta

This is something a little different; one of those pasta dishes like Marmite that you'll either love or hate! If you love jerk seasoning, then it will be a treat for you. I absolutely love it. This is another pasta dish that I came up with by accident – I had some jerk seasoning, some pasta and a little coconut milk in the cupboard, so thought I'd see what happened when I threw them together. I recommend that you use one green, one red and one yellow pepper to make it look extra pretty!

Ingredients

1 tbsp vegetable oil
1 yellow pepper, cut into strips
1 red pepper cut into strips
1 green pepper cut into strips
5 spring onions, finely sliced (keep the green parts to serve)
4 garlic cloves, minced
2 tbsp jerk seasoning
400g tin coconut milk
300g rigatoni (or other pasta)
salt and black pepper

Method

1. Put a pan over a medium heat and add the vegetable oil along with the peppers and the white parts of the spring onions. Let this cook for 2 minutes.
2. Add the garlic and continue to cook for 1 minute. Then add the jerk seasoning and stir for 30 seconds.
3. Pour in the coconut milk and give everything a good stir. Turn the heat down to low and let the sauce bubble away while you cook the pasta.
4. Bring a saucepan of salted water to the boil and cook the pasta according to the packet instructions, then drain.
5. Spoon the pasta into the sauce, which should have slightly reduced and thickened at this point. Mix through and toss if you like.
6. Taste the sauce and add salt and black pepper if needed (it may be quite salty because of the jerk seasoning).
7. Sprinkle with the green slices of spring onions and serve.

IN THE BASKET

Spring onions:
based on a 100g bunch

Garlic: based on a whole bulb

Jerk seasoning:
based on a 100g tub

Pasta: based on a 500g packet

Puttanesca Spaghetti

Who knew that budget food could taste this good? The flavours in this pasta dish will astonish you. It's absolutely delicious! Every time I eat it, I feel as though I've had about ten energy drinks; it makes me feel so alive! This really is a dish to look forward to – quick, cheap, easy and incredibly tasty.

Ingredients

- 2 tbsp olive oil
- 8 tinned anchovies, cut into small pieces, plus 2 tsp juice from the tin
- 4 garlic cloves, finely chopped
- ½ tsp chilli flakes
- 2 tbsp capers
- 400g tin chopped tomatoes
- 300g spaghetti
- 80g black pitted olives
- handful of fresh parsley, finely chopped (optional)
- salt and black pepper

Method

1. Put a pan over a low heat pan and add the oil, anchovies, garlic, chilli flakes and capers. Let them cook for 2 minutes.
2. Pour in the tomatoes, give everything a stir and allow the mixture to simmer on a low heat while you cook the spaghetti.
3. Bring a pan of salted water to the boil and cook the spaghetti according to the packet instructions. Then drain, reserving some of the cooking water.
4. Add the cooked spaghetti to the sauce along with half a ladle (about 50ml) of the cooking water to loosen it.
5. Toss everything together in the pan and add the olives.
6. Add a crack of black pepper and stir through the parsley, if using.

🗑 IN THE BASKET

Anchovies: based on a 50g tin

Garlic: based on a whole bulb

Chilli flakes: based on a 29g jar

Capers: based on a 100g jar

Spaghetti: based on a 500g packet

Olives: based on a 340g jar

Burgers, Sandwiches and Toasties

52

58

Pesto and Salami Grilled Cheese Sandwich

I love a grilled cheese sandwich, but this recipe takes it to another level with added pesto and salami. This is a great combination that works brilliantly for breakfast, brunch or a sandwich lunch! When making a grilled cheese sandwich it's important to have the griddle pan on a medium to low heat, rather than a high heat. This allows the bread to toast as well as giving the cheese long enough to melt and become oozy without burning the bread

Ingredients

8 thick slices tiger or
    bloomer bread
2 tbsp green pesto
16 slices salami, chorizo
    or pepperoni
160g grated mozzarella
black pepper

Method

1. Heat a griddle pan on a medium low heat and put 2 slices of bread in it. Cook for 1½–2 minutes until they are toasted to your liking.
2. Flip over the slices and spread ½ tablespoon of pesto on 1 slice, followed by 4 slices of salami, a quarter of the grated mozzarella and a crack of black pepper.
3. Lay the second slice of bread on top and cook, keeping a close eye on it. It will take a maximum of 2 minutes for the cheese to melt and the bread to be nicely toasted.
4. Repeat with the remaining bread and filling to make the rest of the sandwiches.

IN THE BASKET

Bread: based on a 400g
tiger loaf

Pesto: based on a 190g jar

Mozzarella: based on a
250g packet

Salami: based on a 135g packet

Sloppy Joes

These are messy to eat, but they're worth every single bite. I've kept them as simple, cheap and quick to make as possible. The recipe is a quick chilli slapped between two buns. The chilli con carne seasoning is not particularly traditional, but I think it takes the recipe to another level. If you don't have any, you can make your own from half a teaspoon of ground cumin, a teaspoon each of paprika and chilli powder, half a teaspoon each of oregano and ground coriander and half a teaspoon each of garlic powder and onion powder. Don't knock it until you've tried it – this is a proper treat!

Ingredients

1 tbsp olive or vegetable oil
1 onion, finely chopped
1 pepper, finely chopped
4 garlic cloves, minced
500g 20% fat minced beef
41g packet chilli con carne
   seasoning
400g tin chopped tomatoes
4 burger buns (brioche or seeded)
4 American cheese slices
   (optional)
salt and black pepper

Method

1. Put a pan on a medium heat and pour in the oil. Add the onion and pepper and cook for 2 minutes, stirring continuously. Put aside 2 teaspoons of the mixture to serve.

2. Add the garlic and cook for a further minute, then the beef. Break up the mince in the pan with the back of a wooden spoon or whisk so the pieces of meat are as small as possible.

3. Brown the meat and add the chilli seasoning along with salt and pepper to taste. Cook for a further minute.

4. Add the tomatoes, lower the heat and let the mixture bubble away for 5 minutes. Keep your eye on it and give it a stir every minute to ensure nothing sticks to the pan.

5. Toast the buns and put a slice of American cheese on each one. Divide the chilli beef mixture equally among the buns and finish with a sprinkling of the reserved onion and pepper.

IN THE BASKET

Garlic: based on a whole bulb

Cheese slices: based on a
255g pack

Grilled Chicken, Bacon and Cheese Sandwich

This is my favourite sandwich, so I just had to include it! It's so simple, but delivers comforting, heavenly mouthfuls every time. I've been eating it for years and never tire of it. I use sliced cooked chicken to save time and because it is cheap. The saltiness of the bacon, the mature Cheddar, the crunch of spring onion and the sour cream all come together for a sandwich that is a real treat.

Ingredients

300g bacon, chopped into 1cm chunks

100g cooked sliced chicken, cut into 1cm chunks

150g mature Cheddar, grated

3 spring onions (green part only), thinly sliced

200g sour cream

8 thick slices tiger or bloomer bread

black pepper

Method

1. Put the bacon pieces into a cold pan and bring the heat up slowly to render the fat. Let the bacon cook for 4–5 minutes until the pieces are crispy then take them out and drain them on a piece of kitchen paper.

2. Combine the chicken, Cheddar, spring onions, sour cream, bacon pieces and a crack of black pepper in a mixing bowl. Mix everything together until well combined.

3. Put a griddle pan on a medium heat, add 2 slices of bread and toast them for 2 minutes. Flip 1 slice and top it with a quarter of the cheesy chicken bacon mixture. Put the other slice on top (with the toasted side on the filling) and cook for a further minute and a half on both sides.

4. Repeat with the remaining slices of bread and filling. When all the sandwiches are cooked, slice them in half and serve.

IN THE BASKET

Spring onions: based on a 100g bunch

Cheese: based on a 250g block

Bread: based on a 400g tiger loaf

Spicy Chorizo Cheesy Beans on Toast

Are you British if you've never eaten beans on toast? It's a national dish I absolutely love: a true British budget classic. This recipe breaks with tradition, adding chorizo and hot and spicy chilli seasoning – and then melts mozzarella into it for some brilliant cheese pulls. The beauty of it is that it's still within the budget! I suggest you buy ready-sliced chorizo as chorizo rings are too expensive!

Ingredients

1 tbsp vegetable oil
½ onion, finely diced
70g pack thinly sliced chorizo
2 garlic cloves, minced
41g packet chilli con carne
    seasoning (see page 62 for how
    to make your own)
400g tin chopped tomatoes
2 x 400g tins haricot beans
125g ball mozzarella
8 slices tiger or bloomer bread
8 pickled jalapeño slices, to
    serve (optional)
salt and black pepper

Method

1. Put a pan on a medium heat and add the oil, onion and sliced chorizo. Let them cook for 3–4 minutes until the onion begins to soften. Add the garlic and continue to cook for a further minute, stirring continuously.

2. Tip in the seasoning and mix it through, then cook for a further 30 seconds. Add the tomatoes and haricot beans, and then half fill one of the tins with cold water and pour that in too.

3. Mix everything well and then let it bubble away for 10–15 minutes until the sauce has reduced and thickened. In the final couple of minutes, break up the ball of mozzarella and mix it through until it melts.

4. Meanwhile, toast the slices of bread (ideally in a griddle pan to give them black char marks – alternatively use a toaster). Finish the beans with salt and black pepper to taste.

5. Plate up, spooning the beans over the toast and topping them with pickled jalapeños, if using.

IN THE BASKET

Garlic: based on a whole bulb

Bread: based on a 400g tiger loaf

Jalapenos: based on a 200g jar

Cheesy Meatball Marinara Subs

Give Subway a run for their money with these incredibly easy and cheap meatball marinara subs! Making your own meatballs keeps costs right down, but if you're feeling lazy or rich then of course you can spend a little more and buy some. Making your own marinara sauce couldn't be simpler. If you want to add little extras to the sauce, such as chilli flakes, feel free to do so. When making these, I cut the ends off each sub roll and blitz them in a food processor to make breadcrumbs. You need the equivalent of one slice of bread. You'll absolutely love these!

Ingredients

For the marinara sauce

3 tbsp olive oil

½ onion, finely diced

2 garlic cloves, minced

400g tins chopped tomatoes

10 fresh basil leaves, plus extra to serve

salt and black pepper

For the meatballs

500g 20% fat minced beef

1 onion, grated

4 garlic cloves, minced

40g breadcrumbs

2 tbsp olive oil, plus extra for frying

handful of grated Parmesan (optional)

1 tsp dried oregano (optional)

For the subs

125g ball mozzarella

4 sub rolls

Method

1. Start by making the marinara sauce. Put a pot on a low heat and add the oil, onion and garlic. Let them soften for 2 minutes, then add the tomatoes, half fill one of the tins with water and add that. Add the basil leaves and some salt and pepper, give it all a good stir and let the sauce bubble away on a low heat while you prep the meatballs.

2. Grab a large mixing bowl and mix together the minced beef, onion, garlic, breadcrumbs, oil with salt and black pepper to taste. Add the Parmesan or a little oregano, if using, which will make the meatballs even tastier. Don't be afraid to use your hands to make sure that everything is nicely combined.

3. Roll your balls; I go for golf ball size but you can make them as big or small as you like. Just be aware that the bigger they are, the longer they take to cook. I recommend wetting your hands with cold water before you start rolling, to stop the meat sticking to your fingers!

4. When you've rolled all the meatballs, put a pan over a high heat, pour in the oil and put the balls in the pan. Sear them all over until they brown. You don't need to cook them through at this point, just to colour them.

5. Take the meatballs out of the pan and wipe it down. Lower the heat and transfer the marinara sauce to the pan. Replace the meatballs, put on the lid and let everything bubble away on a low heat for 5 minutes to finish cooking the meatballs in the sauce.

6. Break up the mozzarella ball and spread it evenly across the rolls. Heat the grill to hot then put the rolls under the grill to melt the cheese and slightly toast the bread for 2 minutes maximum.

7. Now bring everything together – place the meatballs on the rolls and spoon over the marinara sauce. Sprinkle over a little finely chopped basil and serve.

 **IN THE BASKET**

Garlic: based on a whole bulb

Basil: based on a 30g packet

Family Fish Finger Sandwich

I'm introducing the family fish finger sandwich; this will easily feed four people and I've even included batter bits! You'll feel as though you've been to the gym just lifting this off the worktop – don't forget to put on your safety boots before trying to manoeuvre it around the kitchen! If you love a fish finger sandwich as much as I do, then you're going to love this recipe. The sauces are optional extras as I know they divide opinion – my favourite accompaniments are tartar sauce on the bottom bun and ketchup spread across the top bun. I have no idea how you'll manage to fit it into your mouth, but I'll let you figure that out!

Ingredients

500g plain flour
250–300ml cold tap water
500g frozen fish fillets (transfer to the fridge the day before cooking)
750ml vegetable oil, for deep frying
400g round cob loaf
sauces (such as tartar sauce or ketchup) (optional)
1 iceberg lettuce, shredded
salt and black pepper

Method

1. Divide the flour equally between 2 mixing bowls. Season both bowls with salt and pepper to taste. Gradually pour the water into one of the bowls while continuously mixing to form a batter. It should be the consistency of paint. For even better results you can use sparkling water or beer instead of tap water.

2. Put the fish fillets one at a time into the seasoned flour and then submerge them in the batter.

3. Heat a deep-fat fryer to 190°C and cook the fish in batches. If you don't have a deep-fat fryer, heat some vegetable oil in a pot and check the temperature with a thermometer. Carefully lower the fish pieces into the hot oil so the batter slightly sets and doesn't stick to the fryer basket.

4. Cook the fish for 3–4 minutes in the hot oil. The batter should be golden brown and crispy. Season the fish with salt when you take it out of the fryer.

5. Slice the loaf in half horizontally and toast it lightly in a griddle pan.

6. Assemble the sandwich as follows: spread the toasted bottom of the loaf with tartar sauce, follow with lettuce and then the fish. Add a squeeze of ketchup followed by the top of the loaf and then cut the loaf into quarters.

Onion Bhaji Burgers

I love an onion bhaji or two – so let's whip up a big batch, stick them on some beautifully toasted brioche buns and top them with some mint yoghurt. A combination to die for! Traditionally you'd use gram (chickpea) flour, but I've used plain flour as its cheaper and more readily available.

Ingredients

200g plain flour
2 heaped tbsp curry powder
250ml cold tap water
3 onions, thinly sliced
1 red chilli, finely chopped, plus
    extra to serve
4 garlic cloves, finely chopped
10g fresh coriander, finely
    chopped, plus extra to serve
750ml vegetable oil, for
    deep frying
200ml plain yoghurt
10g fresh mint, finely chopped
juice of ½ lemon
4 brioche buns
salt and black pepper

Method

1. Put the flour, curry powder, some salt and pepper and the tap water into a large mixing bowl and mix them together until you have a smooth batter.
2. Add the onion, chilli, garlic and coriander. Mix thoroughly, ensuring that everything is seasoned. Don't be afraid to use your hands.
3. Set your deep-fat fryer to 180°C or heat some vegetable oil in a pot and check the temperature with a thermometer. Scoop up a heaped tablespoon of the onion mixture at a time and carefully put it into the hot oil. Fry the bhajis in batches for 3–4 minutes until they are golden and crispy. When they are cooked, put them on kitchen paper to soak up any excess oil.
4. While the bhajis are frying, combine the yoghurt, mint and lemon juice in a bowl and toast the buns. I toast my buns in a griddle pan to give them charred bar marks. Toast both the top and bottom of the buns.
5. Build the burgers starting with the bottom half of a bun, adding mint yoghurt, then the bhajis (you can usually fit 3 of them in a bun depending on how big you've made them). Follow with more mint yoghurt and finely chopped chill, followed by a sprinkling of coriander.

IN THE BASKET

Flour: based on a 500g bag

Curry powder: based
on an 85g tub

Chillies: based on a 65g packet

Garlic: based on a whole bulb

Coriander: based on a 30g packet

Yoghurt: based on a 500ml tub

Mint: based on a 30g packet

Super Simple Smash Burgers

The beauty of smash burgers is that they cook quickly so they're perfect for a midweek meal. I like to add some thinly sliced onions to the patty when smashing it down so you end up with caramelised onions throughout a beautifully seared patty. You can add or remove whatever you like from this burger – it really is versatile. Some crispy streaky bacon is a great addition (if you're feeling rich), or some pickles or even a fried egg. Then top it with your favourite sauce. The possibilities are endless.

Ingredients

4 seeded burger buns, halved
500g 20% fat minced beef
sprinkling of garlic powder and
    onion powder (optional)
½ tbsp vegetable oil
½ onion, thinly sliced
8 burger cheese slices
sauces (ketchup, mustard,
    burger sauce)
iceberg lettuce leaves
2 tomatoes, sliced
salt and black pepper

IN THE BASKET

Cheese slices: based on a
255g pack

Lettuce: based on a whole lettuce

Method

1. First toast the burger buns in a toaster or on a griddle pan. I like to get this out of the way first so you can focus on the burgers.

2. Put the minced beef into a mixing bowl and season it generously with salt and black pepper. Add a little garlic powder and onion powder here, if using. Use your hands to squeeze the meat and ensure that it is seasoned throughout.

3. Divide the beef into 4 equal chunks and roll them into balls.

4. Heat a pan until it is screaming hot and add the oil followed by 2 of the balls of beef. You could add more balls if you can fit them into your pan.

5. Press the burgers flat as hard as you can. A burger press is ideal, but if you don't have one place a piece of baking paper on top of the beef ball and press it flat with a spatula (the baking paper will prevent the meat sticking to the spatula).

6. Add some onion slices to each patty and press them again to infuse the onions into the burger.

7. After 2 minutes of cooking over a high heat, flip the burgers. They should be crispy, brown and seared on one side.

8. Place 2 squares of cheese on each patty and cook the burgers for 2 minutes on the other side. They should be beautifully seared with nicely melted cheese.

9. Build the burgers starting from the bottom half of a bun, adding sauce of your choice, some lettuce, tomato slices, a patty, more sauce and finally the top half of the bun.

Chilli Cheese Dogs with Crispy Onions

This offers great value for money – you can make six fully loaded mixed bean chilli dogs for a fiver and they really do taste like the real deal. I use tinned hot dog frankfurters, but feel free to use a different type of sausage. You can make your own chilli seasoning from half a teaspoon of ground cumin, a teaspoon each of paprika and chilli powder, half a teaspoon each of oregano and ground coriander and half a teaspoon each of garlic powder and onion powder. There will be enough chilli left over to have the following day on a jacket spud or with some rice. These are a great addition to any buffet or party food platter – and the cheese pulls are a thing of beauty!

Ingredients

- 2 tbsp vegetable oil, plus 300ml for deep frying
- 2 onions, 1½ finely diced, the other ½ thinly sliced
- 4 garlic cloves, minced
- 41g packet chilli con carne seasoning
- 400g tin chopped tomatoes
- 400g tin mixed beans (kidney, black-eyed, borlotti and haricot beans, plus sweetcorn)
- 400g tin hot dog sausages (8 hot dogs), drained
- 125g ball mozzarella
- 6 finger rolls or hot dog buns, halved
- 3 spring onions, finely chopped, to serve (optional)
- salt and black pepper

Method

1. Start by putting a pan on a medium heat and pouring in 2 tablespoons of the oil, then add the finely diced onion and a pinch of salt. Let the onions soften for 2–3 minutes, then add the garlic and continue to cook for 1 minute.

2. Add the chilli seasoning and continue to cook for 30 seconds, then pour in the tomatoes and the mixed beans. Half fill one of the tins with cold water and tip that in as well.

3. Mix everything together, turn the heat down to low and let the chilli sauce simmer for 5–6 minutes. Keep your eye on it and stir it regularly to ensure that nothing sticks to bottom of the the pan.

4. Meanwhile heat 300ml of oil in another pan on a low heat and add the sliced onion to make the crispy onions (or if you have a deep-fat fryer, you could use that). Fry the onion slices gently for 8–10 minutes. Keep the heat low so they don't burn and go bitter. When they are golden brown, take them out of the oil and drain them on kitchen paper.

5. While the onion slices are frying, put a griddle pan on a high heat and add the hot dogs. Let them cook for 3–4 minutes. You want griddle bar marks across each sausage.

6. When the sausages are cooked, put them into the finger rolls or hot dog buns. There are 8 sausages per tin so cut up the remaining 2 sausages and get them into the buns too. Don't waste anything!

7. By this point the chilli sauce will have thickened. Arrange the hot dogs on a baking tray and spoon the chilli sauce over them generously. Heat the grill to high, break the ball of mozzarella into small chunks and scatter them over the hot dogs. Put the tray under the hot grill for 2 minutes – just long enough to melt the mozzarella.

8. Serve each hot dog with the spring onions, if using, and some crispy onions.

IN THE BASKET

Garlic: based on a whole bulb

Spring onions: based on a 100g bunch

BLT Fritter Burgers

I love a bacon, lettuce and tomato sandwich. But I also love a sweetcorn fritter. So I have combined the two to make the ultimate budget burger! I mix crispy bacon bits through the fritter batter with the sweetcorn and spring onions for some crisp pops of flavour – a proper treat! It may take a couple of attempts to perfect the cooking of the fritters, so I've ensured that there is plenty of batter in this recipe to allow for any mishaps! Don't be disheartened if your first attempt doesn't go to plan, because when you get them right you'll want to make them time and time again. They're good enough to eat on their own!

Ingredients

4 slices bacon, cut into
   1cm chunks
200g self-raising flour
220ml cold tap water
3 spring onions, finely sliced
140g tin sweetcorn, drained
½ red chilli, deseeded
8 tbsp vegetable oil
4 seeded burger buns, halved
sauces, such as sweet chilli,
   to serve (optional)
½ iceberg lettuce, shredded
2 tomatoes, sliced into rounds
salt and black pepper

IN THE BASKET

Bacon: based on a pack of 8 slices

Flour: based on a 500g bag

Spring onions: based on a
100g bunch

Chillies: based on a 65g packet

Lettuce: based on a whole lettuce

Method

1. Start by putting the bacon pieces into a cold pan, then bring up the heat gradually to render the fat. You're aiming to cook it until it's nice and crispy. It will take 4–5 minutes. Take the cooked bacon pieces out of the pan and drain them on some kitchen paper.

2. While the bacon is cooking, put the self-raising flour into a mixing bowl and gradually add the water while mixing constantly. Mix until a smooth batter is formed.

3. Add the spring onions, sweetcorn, chilli, crispy cooked bacon and a crack of black pepper. Mix everything together.

4. Put 2 burger-sized, round cookie cutters into a pan over a medium heat and pour a tablespoon of oil into each one.

5. Put 2 dessertspoons of batter into each cookie cutter and work it into the shape of the mould. It will begin to rise almost immediately. After 30 seconds, carefully remove the moulds (the fritters should hold their shape) and cook the fritters for 2 minutes on each side or until they are golden brown and crispy. Repeat with the remaining batter (the quantities allow 2 fritters per bun).

6. Toast the buns and assemble everything. Start with the bottom of each bun, followed by some sauce, lettuce, tomato slices, 2 fritters, more sauce and finally the top of the bun.

One-pan
Meals

72

83

76

88

Sweet Potato Hash

I love a good one-pan meal for two reasons; first, they are simple and second, you only have to wash up one pan when you've finished cooking! This is a super simple hash that you can complete within 30 minutes – suitable for breakfast, brunch or even tea time!

Ingredients

2 tbsp vegetable or olive oil

1kg sweet potatoes, diced into
   1cm pieces

1 red pepper, diced into
   1cm pieces

1 red onion, finely chopped

4 garlic cloves, minced

50g spinach

1 tsp chilli powder

4 medium eggs

1 avocado, sliced, to serve

salt and black pepper

Method

1. Put a large, lidded pan on a medium heat, then add the oil and the sweet potato. Cook for 8–10 minutes until the potatoes are fork tender.

2. Add the pepper, onion and garlic and continue to cook for about 2 minutes. Then add the spinach, salt and black pepper to taste and the chilli powder. Give everything a stir until the spinach begins to wilt.

3. Make 4 wells or dips in the potato mixture and crack an egg into each one. Put the lid on the pan to steam and cook the eggs for 3–4 minutes, or until they are cooked to your liking. Ideally, the egg yolks will be beautifully runny.

4. Take the pan off the heat, grind a bit more black pepper over the eggs to finish and serve with the avocado slices.

IN THE BASKET

Garlic: based on a whole bulb

Chilli powder: based on a 40g jar

Spinach: based on a 240g packet

Eggs: based on a box of 6

Breakfast Hash

This is an amazingly simple four-ingredient breakfast hash
(not including salt and pepper). It's the way I want to start
every day. Crispy bacon and potatoes topped with runny yolk
fried eggs, with a touch of freshness from the spring onions.
A little treat that will set you up for the day.

Ingredients

8 slices smoked bacon, cut into
  2cm pieces
4 baking potatoes, skin on,
  cut into 1.4cm chunks
5 spring onions, finely sliced,
  white and green parts separated
4 medium eggs
salt and black pepper

Method

1. Put the bacon pieces into a cold dry pan and bring the heat up
   gradually. Let the bacon cook for 4–5 minutes until it is crispy and
   has released all its fat. Take the bacon out and set it aside but retain
   the juices and fat in the pan.

2. Put the potato chunks into the pan and cook them in the bacon fat
   for 5 minutes on a high heat to give them a golden colour. Ensure
   they brown on all sides by flipping them over with a spatula.

3. Turn down the heat and then cook for 10 more minutes until the
   potatoes soften, turning them regularly. Add the whites of the spring
   onions and cook for 1 minute.

4. Return the bacon to the pan, give everything a mix and then take
   it all out of the pan and set it aside. The hash might be quite salty
   because of the bacon, but taste it and season with salt and black
   pepper if needed.

5. Crack the eggs into the empty pan and cook them as you like them –
   ideally with a nice runny yolk!

6. Plate up the hash and top each plate with a fried egg, a crack of
   black pepper and the spring onion greens.

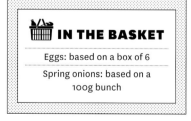

IN THE BASKET

Eggs: based on a box of 6

Spring onions: based on a
100g bunch

Chickpea Shakshuka

Eggs can be expensive these days, so in this recipe I've swapped them for chickpeas. This makes such a warm, wholesome breakfast and it's perfect for a cold morning. Serve it with lots of crusty bread to dip into it.

Ingredients

2 tbsp vegetable oil
1 onion, diced
1 red pepper, diced
4 garlic cloves, finely chopped
2 tsp paprika
1 tsp ground cumin
2 x 400g tins chopped tomatoes
2 x 400g tins chickpeas, drained
handful of fresh parsley, finely
   chopped
crusty bread, to serve
salt and black pepper

Method

1. Put a pan on a medium heat pan and add the oil, onion, pepper and a pinch of salt. Let this cook and soften for 3–4 minutes, then add the garlic and cook for a further minute.
2. Add the paprika and cumin and stir them through for 30 seconds. Pour in the tomatoes and chickpeas, give everything a good mix and let the sauce bubble away on a low heat for 5 minutes.
3. Taste and add salt and black pepper.
4. Sprinkle over the parsley and serve with the bread for dipping.

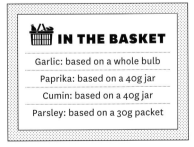

IN THE BASKET

Garlic: based on a whole bulb

Paprika: based on a 40g jar

Cumin: based on a 40g jar

Parsley: based on a 30g packet

Veggie Stir-fry

This is a simple stir-fry that you can throw together in 15 minutes! You can mix and match the vegetables and put in pretty much what you like. I use mushrooms, mangetout and carrots, but you could also use peppers, sugar snap peas, Tenderstem broccoli, green beans, beansprouts or other vegetables. The possibilities are endless. Make sure you chop all the fresh ingredients before you start cooking. I've opted for instant ramen noodles, but you could use rice noodles or egg noodles too.

Ingredients

3 x 80g packs dried instant ramen noodles (I use Indomie Mi Goreng)
3 tbsp vegetable oil
300g mushrooms, quartered
1 carrot, cut into thin batons
200g mangetout
5 garlic cloves, finely chopped
1 red chilli, plus extra to serve
thumb-size piece of root ginger, finely chopped
5 tbsp dark soy sauce
juice of ½ lime, plus slices to serve

Method

1. Soak the noodles in some boiling water so they begin to soften.
2. Put a wok or a pan with sloping sides on a high heat and pour in the oil. Add the mushrooms and carrot and cook them for 2 minutes. Try not to move them around too much; you want the mushrooms to take on some colour.
3. Add the mangetout, garlic, chilli and ginger and toss the contents of the pan for a further minute.
4. Add the soy sauce followed by the softened noodles and toss everything together for 30 seconds.
5. Add the lime juice and plate up.
6. Serve with a slice of lime and some finely chopped chilli for a pop of colour.

IN THE BASKET

Garlic: based on a whole bulb

Chillies: based on a 65g packet

Soy sauce: based on a 150ml bottle

Quick Coconut Curried Fish

Fish can be expensive these days, so if you buy it fresh from the fishmongers you will go over budget! I've based this recipe on using a 500g bag of frozen fish fillets that I transfer to the fridge overnight to defrost before cooking. At the time of writing, you can buy these for £2.50. You can throw this recipe together in 20 minutes including prep! Serve it with some rice and you're on to a winner

Ingredients

1 tbsp vegetable oil
1 onion, finely diced
1 red chilli finely diced, plus thin
    slices to serve
3 garlic cloves, minced
15g piece of root ginger,
    finely chopped
2 tbsp curry powder
1 x 400g tin coconut milk
500g frozen fish fillets, defrosted
juice of ½ lime
handful of fresh coriander,
    finely chopped
salt and black pepper

Method

1. Put a pan on a medium heat and add the oil, onion, chilli and a pinch of salt. Let this cook and soften for 3–4 minutes.
2. Add the garlic and ginger and cook for a further minute, then add the curry powder and stir for 30 seconds. Pour in a little tap water (about 50ml) to stop the spices burning and sticking to the pan.
3. Pour in the coconut milk and then add the fish fillets. Bring the pan to a simmer and let it bubble away on a low heat for 5 minutes or until the fish is beautifully tender.
4. Taste, season with salt and black pepper and add the lime juice. Sprinkle over the coriander and serve with the chilli slices.

IN THE BASKET

Chillies: based on a 65g packet

Garlic: based on a whole bulb

Curry powder: based on an 85g tub

Coriander: based on a 30g packet

Breakfast Chorizo, Beans and Eggs

This recipe is a shakshuka and baked beans hybrid with a bit of chorizo thrown in for good measure! It's one of those meals you can put in the centre of the table so everyone can get stuck in. There are runny yolk eggs and cannellini beans in rich tomato sauce and crusty bread for dipping. This is how I like to start my day, any day.

Ingredients

1 tbsp vegetable or olive oil
½ onion, finely chopped
70g pack thinly sliced chorizo, cut into chunks
2 garlic cloves, finely chopped
2 x 400g tins cannellini beans, drained
400g tin chopped tomatoes
6 medium eggs
handful of fresh parsley, finely chopped, to serve (optional)
crusty bread, to serve
salt and black pepper

Method

1. Put the oil, onion and chorizo into a lidded pan over a medium heat pan and cook for 3–4 minutes until the onion begins to soften. Add the garlic and cook for a further minute.
2. Tip in the beans and tomatoes, then half fill one of the tins with tap water and tip that in too. Give everything a stir and allow the mixture to bubble away for 10 minutes on a medium heat.
3. When the sauce has begun to thicken, make 6 wells and crack the eggs into them. Put on the lid and cook on a low heat for about 3–4 minutes (the lid will help to steam and cook the top of the eggs).
4. When the eggs are cooked, season them with salt and black pepper. Sprinkle over the parsley and serve with chunks of crusty bread.

IN THE BASKET

Garlic: based on a whole bulb

Parsley: based on a 30g packet

Veggie Thai Green Curry

This is one of the simplest and quickest curry recipes you'll ever make. You can add any vegetables you like to this curry! Cauliflower and baby corn are a great addition. Just ensure that you cut all the veggies into 2cm bite-sized pieces, so they all cook quickly. You don't want to wait ages for the veggies to soften.

Ingredients

2 tbsp vegetable oil

1 onion, finely diced

1 red chilli, finely chopped, plus
    extra slices to serve

170g jar Thai green curry paste

400g tin coconut milk

2 baking potatoes, peeled and cut
    into 2cm chunks

1 large carrot, peeled and cut into
    2cm chunks

200g green beans, cut in half

zest and juice of ½ lime

20g fresh coriander, finely
    chopped

salt and black pepper

Method

1. Put a lidded pan on a medium heat, add the oil, onion and a pinch of salt and cook for 3–4 minutes until the onion begins to soften. Add the chilli and cook for a further minute.

2. Add the whole jar of curry paste and cook for another minute, then pour in the coconut milk. Half fill the tin with tap water and add that too.

3. Bring the contents of the pan to a simmer and add the potato and carrot. Put on the lid and let everything simmer for 8–10 minutes.

4. Add the beans and simmer for a further 4–5 minutes or until the beans are cooked.

5. Add the lime zest and juice and the coriander and mix them through. Taste and season to taste.

6. Serve with red chilli slices and some rice.

IN THE BASKET

Chillies: based on a 65g packet

Coriander: based on a 30g packet

Skillet Pizzas

I love a good pizza; but do you know what I like even more? A quick and easy pizza. There's no waiting around for dough to rise with this recipe. It's really simple and straightforward! This is a great recipe if you want to get your kids involved in cooking and if they are fussy (as mine are) let them go wild and top the pizzas with whatever they like! I use peppers, pepperoni and red onion, but feel free to substitute other toppings of your choice

MAKES 4 25CM PIZZAS

Ingredients

500g self-raising flour
300ml cold tap water
400g tin chopped tomatoes
1 garlic clove, minced
10 fresh basil leaves, finely
  chopped, plus extra to serve
2 x 125g balls mozzarella
1 red onion, thinly sliced
1 yellow pepper, diced
70g pack thinly sliced pepperoni
salt and black pepper

Method

1. Combine the flour, water and a pinch of salt in a mixing bowl. Mix until they start to form a dough. Lightly flour a board and knead the dough for 2 minutes.
2. Divide the dough into 4 equal portions and roll each to about the thickness of a £1 coin. Each should be at least 25cm in diameter.
3. Combine the tomatoes, garlic and basil in another bowl along with a pinch of salt and some black pepper.
4. Heat a frying pan until it's screaming hot and carefully put in one of the dough pieces. Cook it for 2 minutes, until the bottom of the dough begins to go slightly crisp. You'll see the dough rise slightly.
5. While the dough is in the pan, spoon 4–5 tablespoons of the tomato sauce on top and spread it all over. Break up the mozzarella balls and spread some over the sauce and then top with the onion, pepper pieces and pepperoni slices.
6. Heat the grill to a high temperature then put the pan underneath for 3–4 minutes until the mozzarella has turned beautifully golden.
7. Remove the pizza and repeat with the remaining 3 pieces of dough – or you can freeze the dough and save it for whenever you fancy eating pizza!
8. Cut the pizzas into quarters and serve with the basil leaves.

IN THE BASKET

Garlic: based on a whole bulb

Basil: based on a 30g packet

Chilli Garlic Noodles

I've always believed that you measure garlic with your heart and not your head. If your head tells you to add three cloves, your heart will come back with a counteroffer to use ten. This is exactly what you need to do with this recipe! My heart told me to add an entire bulb and I had to oblige! This is the ultimate way to turn some ordinary ramen noodles into something amazingly tasty, topped with a fried egg with a runny yolk and a crisp bottom. It's a bit of heaven on a plate for very little money.

Ingredients

4 x 80g packs dried instant ramen noodles (or other noodles)
2 tbsp vegetable oil, plus extra for frying the eggs
1 bulb garlic, cloves finely chopped
2 chillies, deseeded and finely chopped
5 tbsp dark soy sauce
6 spring onions (green part only), finely sliced
4 medium eggs
black pepper

Method

1. Put the noodles into boiling water to soak and soften.
2. Meanwhile, put a pan on a low heat and add the vegetable oil, garlic and chilli. Cook for 2 minutes until the mixture becomes fragrant.
3. Turn up the heat and add the soy sauce, then let it bubble away for a minute.
4. Add the softened noodles and spring onions and toss everything together in the pan for 1 minute until nicely combined. Turn off the heat and set the pan aside.
5. In a separate pan, cook the fried eggs. I like a crispy bottom and a runny yolk so I cook them in oil on a high heat.
6. Serve the noodles topped with the fried eggs. Finish the eggs with a crack of black pepper.

IN THE BASKET

Chillies: based on a 65g packet

Soy sauce: based on a 150ml bottle

Spring onions: based on a 100g bunch

Eggs: based on a box of 6

Chickpea Curry

This is a great curry for vegetarians or vegans; I enjoy a tin of chickpeas from time to time – they're great in salads, stews and so on. But they're even better in a curry! This curry is pretty basic, but very adaptable and you could also make it with vegetables or even some chicken. Serve this with rice or naan bread, or even put it on a jacket spud.

Ingredients

2 tbsp vegetable oil
2 onions, finely chopped
1 chilli, deseeded and
    finely chopped
6 garlic cloves, finely chopped
thumb-size piece of root ginger,
    finely chopped
3 tbsp curry powder
400g tin tomatoes
300ml tap water
2 x 400g tins chickpeas, drained
20g bunch of fresh coriander,
    finely chopped
salt and black pepper

Method

1. Put the oil in a pan over a medium heat and add the onions and chilli with a pinch of salt. Cook them for 5 minutes.

2. Add the garlic and ginger and cook for a further 2 minutes. Add the curry powder, stir and cook for a further 30 seconds, then add a little tap water to stop the spices sticking.

3. Add the tomatoes, give everything a stir, let it bubble away for 2 minutes and then add the water. At this point you can blend it to make a smooth sauce or you can simply leave it as it is.

4. Add the chickpeas and simmer on a low heat for 5 minutes. Taste and add salt and black pepper to taste. Scatter over the coriander and serve.

🧺 IN THE BASKET

Chillies: based on a 65g packet

Garlic: based on a whole bulb

Curry powder: based on an 85g tub

Coriander: based on a 30g packet

Fish Stew with Croutons

This is another easy fish dish that takes 20 minutes to cook, including prep! There's a lot going on in this pan, with flaky fish, a rich tomato-based sauce, crunchy croutons and hearty vegetables. It ticks all the boxes for a proper winter warmer! To keep within budget, the recipe uses frozen fish fillets, which should be defrosted in the fridge overnight.

Ingredients

4–5 tbsp vegetable oil
1 crusty roll, cut into 2cm chunks
1 courgette, roughly chopped
1 red onion, roughly chopped
1 yellow pepper, roughly chopped
3 garlic cloves, finely chopped
½ tsp chilli powder
400g tin chopped tomatoes
500g frozen fish fillets, defrosted
juice of ½ lemon, plus slices
   to serve
handful of fresh parsley,
   finely chopped
salt and black pepper

Method

1. Start by cooking the croutons. Pour 4 tablespoons of the oil into a hot pan and add the chopped rolls. Crisp them in the hot oil, turning them regularly until they are golden all over. When crisp, take them out and set them aside.

2. Wipe the pan and pour in a tablespoon of oil, then add the courgette, onion, pepper and a pinch of salt. Let this mixture soften for 2–3 minutes, then add the garlic and chilli powder and continue to cook for 1 minute.

3. Pour in the tomatoes, then half fill the tin with water and add that too (you could use chicken stock here instead of water to add extra flavour). Bring the sauce to a simmer and then add the fish.

4. Simmer on a low heat for 5 minutes, or until the fish is beautifully flaky. Poaching the fish in the pan will give the sauce a fishy flavour!

5. Add the lemon juice, taste, and add salt and black pepper if needed.

6. Top with the lemon slices and parsley, then scatter the croutons over the top to serve.

IN THE BASKET

Garlic: based on a whole bulb

Chilli powder: based on a 40g jar

Parsley: based on a 30g packet

Budget
Meaty
Meals

94

96

Mediterranean Sausage Traybake

Traybakes are the ultimate solution to dinner in a busy household. Just chop up a few ingredients, put them on a baking tray and stick it in the oven. You'll have a tasty, easy and quick dinner sorted! If you want to make this even more delicious and you can spend a bit more than usual, you could serve the finished dish with some finely chopped olives or even crumble over a bit of feta cheese. If you can't find Mediterranean vegetable seasoning, you can make your own from a tablespoon each of mixed herbs and paprika and a teaspoon each of ground cumin, garlic powder and onion powder.

Ingredients

1 red onion, chopped into
  3cm chunks
8 pork sausages
1 courgette, cut into ½cm discs
330g cherry tomatoes
1 yellow pepper, cut into
  3cm chunks
4 garlic cloves, finely chopped
30g packet Mediterranean
  vegetable seasoning
5 tbsp olive oil
handful of fresh basil or parsley,
  finely chopped (optional)
salt and black pepper

Method

1. Preheat the oven to 180°C/160°C fan/gas mark 4.
2. Put the onion, sausages, courgette, tomatoes, pepper, garlic, seasoning and salt and pepper on a baking tray and pour over the oil. Make sure that everything is coated in the oil and seasoning. Ensure that the sausages sit on top of the vegetables so they go nice and brown when cooking.
3. Place the baking tray in the oven and cook for 25 minutes.
4. Serve with the basil or parsley, if using.

IN THE BASKET

Garlic: based on a whole bulb

Paprika Pork Schnitzels and Fries

These beautifully crispy breaded pork steaks are accompanied by possibly the easiest skin-on fries you've ever made. Serve them with your favourite sauce and you're on to a winner. My kids believe they are massive chicken nuggets! Put the fries straight into hot oil for speed – there's no need to parboil. This can all be chucked together in half an hour so it makes a great midweek meal if you fancy a treat!

Ingredients

750ml vegetable oil, for deep frying, plus 200ml to fry the steaks

4 baking potatoes, skin on, cut into fries

2 tsp paprika

80g plain flour

2 eggs

200g golden breadcrumbs

4 pork steaks

sauce or ketchup, to serve

lemon wedges, to serve (optional)

handful of fresh parsley, finely chopped, to serve (optional)

salt and black pepper

Method

1. Heat a deep-fat fryer to 180°C or heat some vegetable oil in a pot and check the temperature with a thermometer. Cook the fries for 15–20 minutes or until they are golden and crispy. When they are cooked, tip them into a bowl and season with salt, pepper and 1 teaspoon of paprika. Toss them in the bowl to coat them evenly.

2. While the fries are cooking, set up 3 bowls. In the first bowl put flour, a teaspoon of paprika and salt and black pepper and mix well. Crack the eggs into the second bowl and whisk them until smooth. Tip the golden breadcrumbs into the third bowl. You now have a 3-stage production line to coat the steaks.

3. Trim any white fat off the steaks and season them with salt and black pepper. Then sandwich them between 2 pieces of cling film or baking paper and bash them with a rolling pin or the bottom of a pan until they are half a centimetre thick. The thinner they are, the faster they will cook.

4. Dredge the steaks in the flour first, then dip them into the beaten egg and finally cover them with the breadcrumbs. Ensure that they are coated evenly and generously all over with breadcrumbs.

5. Heat 200ml of oil in a pan on a medium heat and carefully lay in the steaks. Cook them for 4 minutes on each side until they are golden brown and crispy.

6. Season the steaks with a light sprinkling of salt and serve with the fries and the sauce of your choice, a squeeze of lemon and parsley.

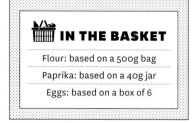

IN THE BASKET

Flour: based on a 500g bag

Paprika: based on a 40g jar

Eggs: based on a box of 6

Quick Meatball Pittas

If you're partial to a meatball this is the recipe for you –
juicy homemade meatballs in pitta with a touch of salad.
These are very tasty and super simple to make. The recipe
is inspired by chippy doner kebabs. I use a doner kebab
seasoning packet to make sure I'm within the budget. If
you can't find this and you have spices and seasonings in
the cupboard, use the following: 1 teaspoon each of onion
powder and garlic powder, ½ teaspoon each of chilli powder
and cinnamon and 1 teaspoon each of paprika and oregano.

Ingredients

500g 20% fat minced beef
½ onion, grated
3 garlic cloves, grated
38g packet doner kebab seasoning
1 red onion, finely chopped
2 tomatoes, finely chopped
½ iceberg lettuce, shredded
juice of ½ lemon
sauces (I like chilli and mint
   yoghurt)
6 pitta breads
salt and black pepper

Method

1. Combine the mince, onion, garlic and packet seasoning in a large
    bowl and add salt and black pepper to taste. Don't be afraid to get
    your hands in the bowl and squeeze everything together until it is all
    well combined.

2. Take small chunks of mixture and roll them into meatballs about the
    size of golf balls. If the meat sticks to your hands, run your hands
    under some cold water.

3. Put a dry pan over a low heat (the fat in the meat means you don't
    need any oil) and add the meatballs. Turn them carefully once every
    1 minute. They will take 8–10 minutes to cook. Baste them frequently
    with the pan juices to keep them moist.

4. Meanwhile, put the onion, tomato and lettuce in a bowl. Add the
    lemon juice and salt and black pepper to taste.

5. If you like your pittas warm, put them in the microwave for about
    30 seconds. Then load up the pittas with salad and meatballs and
    add your chosen sauce.

IN THE BASKET

Garlic: based on a whole bulb

Lettuce: based on a
whole lettuce

Sausage Stroganoff with Mustard Mash

When I was writing this recipe, I wanted to call the dish bangers and mash with a twist. But it's really more like a stroganoff, so I went with that. It's a perfect winter warmer that's quick to make and won't break the bank.

Ingredients

For the mash
4 baking potatoes (about 800g), peeled and cut into 2cm chunks
1 tbsp sour cream
1 tsp French or Dijon mustard
10g fresh parsley, finely chopped
salt and pepper

For the stroganoff
1 tbsp vegetable or olive oil
8 pork sausages
1 onion, finely chopped
4 garlic cloves, finely chopped
1 tsp paprika
1 tbsp plain flour
500ml beef stock (made from a cube)
½ tbsp French or Dijon mustard
1 heaped tbsp sour cream
10g fresh parsley, finely chopped, plus extra to serve
salt and black pepper

Method

1. Start by putting the potatoes into cold salted water and bringing them to the boil.
2. While the potatoes are boiling, put another pan on a high heat and add the oil and the sausages. Sear the sausages until they are brown all over. Take them out of the pan and set them aside. This will take 3–4 minutes – it doesn't matter if they are not cooked through at this point.
3. Lower the heat under the pan to medium, add the onion and a pinch of salt and cook it for 3–4 minutes until it begins to soften. Add the garlic and continue to cook for 1 minute.
4. Add the paprika and mix it through for 30 seconds, then the flour and stir for a further 30 seconds.
5. Pour in the beef stock, followed by the mustard and sour cream. Give everything a good stir. Take the sausages out of the pan and cut each into 4 pieces on an angle, then return them to the pan. Let the sauce bubble away for 5 minutes until it has thickened.
6. By this point the potatoes should be nice and soft. Drain them and add the sour cream, mustard and parsley along with some salt and pepper. Mash the spuds as well as you can – if you like them extra smooth, pass them through a sieve.
7. Taste the stroganoff and add more salt and black pepper if needed. Put a bed of mash on each plate, then add some stroganoff with plenty of sauce. Serve with a sprinkling of parsley.

 **IN THE BASKET**

Sour cream: based on a 150ml pot

Dijon mustard: based on a 200g jar
Parsley: based on a 30g packet
Garlic: based on a whole bulb

Paprika: based on a 40g jar
Flour: based on a 500g bag
Stock cubes: based on a box of 8

Honey Chicken Noodles

This is a great budget dish that ticks all the right boxes on the flavour front! It's spicy, sweet, savoury, garlicky and vibrant. It's difficult to include chicken in budget meals as the price seems to have shot through the roof. Even the cheaper cuts, such as wings and drumsticks, have gone up. This recipe uses a kilo of chicken legs and to keep the cost down, I take the meat off the bones. Legs are tastier than breasts and much cheaper too. If you don't want the work of stripping the meat from the bone, you can use boneless chicken thighs. I use dried ramen noodles as they are really cheap too. This takes no time to throw together and you're going to love it.

Ingredients

2 tbsp vegetable oil

1kg chicken legs, meat cut off
    the bone and chopped into
    2cm pieces

6 garlic cloves, minced

1 red chilli, finely chopped, plus
    extra to serve

thumb-size piece of root ginger,
    finely chopped

1 head broccoli, broken into florets

140g pack dried instant
    ramen noodles

8 tbsp dark soy sauce

2 tbsp honey

salt and black pepper

Method

1. Put a wok or a sloping-sided pan on a high heat and pour in the oil. Add the chicken pieces along with a pinch of salt and black pepper. Let the chicken cook for 3–4 minutes. Try to avoid moving the chicken pieces around the pan – they should be a nice golden colour on both sides.

2. Add the garlic, chilli, ginger and broccoli and continue to cook for 2 minutes. Stir regularly to prevent anything sticking to the bottom of the pan.

3. Meanwhile, soften the noodles in a bowl by covering them with boiling water.

4. Combine the soy sauce and honey in a small bowl and stir. Pour the sauce into the pan and mix everything together. Add the softened noodles and mix everything together. The soy sauce will stain the noodles a nice brown colour.

5. Serve in bowls topped with more chopped chilli.

IN THE BASKET

Garlic: based on a whole bulb

Chillies: based on a 65g packet

Soy sauce: based on a
150ml bottle

Honey: based on a 340g jar

Mini Cajun Chicken Wraps

These days it's difficult to stretch a budget to include chicken in a meal. I've based this recipe on two chicken breasts. These cost just £2.25 at the time of writing. I butterflied the chicken breasts and then cut them into thin strips. To butterfly, place a chicken breast flat on a board and put one hand flat on top. Take a sharp knife and, starting on one side of the breast, carefully cut through it horizontally in a sawing motion so the it opens up like a book. Cutting into strips helps the meat cook more quickly. Have everything at your fingertips before you start for speediness.

Ingredients

200g plain flour
200g plain yoghurt, plus extra
   to serve
30g Cajun seasoning
2 chicken breasts, butterflied and
   cut into thin strips
2 tbsp vegetable or olive oil
2 tomatoes, finely diced
1 red onion, finely diced
juice of ½ lemon
handful of fresh coriander, finely
   chopped, to serve (optional)
salt and black pepper

🗑 IN THE BASKET

Flour: based on a 500g bag

Yoghurt: based on a 500ml tub

Cajun seasoning: based
on a 40g jar

Method

1. Start by making the tortillas. Combine the flour, yoghurt, 1 teaspoon of the Cajun seasoning and a pinch of salt. Bring them all together in the bowl to form a dough.

2. Flour a board and knead the dough for 2 minutes, then cut it into 6 pieces and roll them as thin as you can (about the thickness of a £1 coin). Place a small round bowl on top of the flattened dough and cut round it with a knife. This will give you an ideal mini tortilla circle. Use the offcuts of dough to make another tortilla. Repeat until you have used all the dough.

3. Put a pan on a high heat and put in the tortillas one by one. Cook them for 30 seconds on each side. Repeat until they are all toasted. (You can always buy the tortillas if you can increase your budget. Nothing beats homemade though!)

4. Put the chicken strips into a bowl and add the oil, the remaining Cajun seasoning and salt and black pepper to taste.

5. Put a pan on a high heat, add the chicken and cook for 3–4 minutes. Try to avoid moving them around the pan too much so they colour.

6. Make a salad by combining the tomatoes, onion, salt and black pepper and the lemon juice in a bowl and mixing them together.

7. Serve everything on a board so everyone can dig in, scattering coriander over the top, if using.

8. To assemble the perfect wrap, start with a tortilla, add yoghurt and some salad, then chicken strips, followed by a little more yoghurt and a sprinkling of coriander.

Middle Eastern-inspired Meatballs and Couscous

These days it's difficult to include meat in a budget meal – the cost of the meat alone can be more than a fiver! This means you need to be creative with cheaper cuts of meat. Sausages are a great example. If you choose cheap supermarket sausages and help them along with some extra seasoning and a bit of love, you can turn them into tasty meatballs. I've paired this with couscous, but you could also serve them with rice or eat them with some crusty bread.

Ingredients

8 pork sausages
2 tbsp Middle Eastern seasoning
  (coriander, cumin, onion
  powder, cardamon and chilli
  powder)
1 tbsp vegetable oil
1 red onion, chopped into
  1cm chunks
1 orange pepper, chopped into
  1cm chunks
4 garlic cloves, finely chopped
400g tin chopped tomatoes
20g fresh parsley, finely chopped,
  plus extra to serve
2 x 110g packets couscous
salt and black pepper

IN THE BASKET

Garlic: based on a whole bulb

Middle Eastern seasoning:
based on a 40g jar

Parsley: based on a 30g packet

Method

1. Make an incision down the length of each sausage with a sharp knife, then take the meat out of the sausage skins and put it into a mixing bowl.
2. Season with a tablespoon of the Middle Eastern seasoning and some salt and black pepper. Mix well.
3. Run your hands under the cold tap (to prevent the meat sticking to your hands), break off chunks of meat and roll it into balls. You can make them as big or small as you like; I aim for golf ball size.
4. Put a pan on a medium heat and add the oil along with the meatballs. Cook them until they are golden brown all over, turning them regularly. They don't need to be cooked through at this stage, just browned. When they are coloured all over, take them out and set them aside.
5. Put the onion and pepper into the pan along with a pinch of salt and cook for 2 minutes. Add the garlic along with a tablespoon of the Middle Eastern seasoning and cook for a further minute.
6. Add the tomatoes, then half fill the tin with water and tip that in too.
7. Return the meatballs to the pan and simmer on a low heat for about 10 minutes (or until the meatballs are cooked through and the sauce has reduced).
8. Stir through the parsley, taste, and season with more salt and black pepper if necessary.
9. Heat the couscous according to the packet instructions.
10. Serve the meatballs on a bed of couscous with some extra parsley.

Curried Beef and Potato Bowl

This may not be the prettiest looking dish, but it's filling, cheap and packed full of flavour! If I feel like eating something stodgy and filling, this meal is my go-to dinner. I like to use a Caribbean brand of curry powder for this one (such as Betapac or Dunn's River). I feel that it works well with the minced beef and potatoes. This is quite a subtly spiced dish, but you can spice it up by increasing the quantity of chillies and leaving in the seeds.

Ingredients

2 tbsp vegetable oil

5 spring onions, sliced, green parts to serve

20g piece of root ginger, finely chopped

1 red chilli, deseeded and finely chopped, plus extra slices to serve

4 garlic cloves, finely chopped

500g 20% fat minced beef

2 tbsp Caribbean or Jamaican curry powder

3 baking potatoes, skin on, cut into 2cm cubes

600ml boiling water

salt and black pepper

Method

1. Put a lidded pan on a medium heat and add the oil, spring onions, ginger and chilli with a pinch of salt, then cook for 1 minute. Add the garlic and continue to cook for 1 more minute.

2. Add the mince and break it up with a wooden spoon; you don't want big chunks in the pan. Season the meat with salt and black pepper and cook it until it is browned all over. Add the curry powder and mix for a further minute.

3. Add the potato and then cover with the boiling water. Put on the pan lid and cook for 10 minutes on a low heat.

4. Take off the lid and then cook for a further 3–4 minutes to reduce the sauce. You'll notice it thicken as the potatoes soften.

5. Taste and add more salt and pepper if necessary, then serve with the green spring onions and the chilli slices.

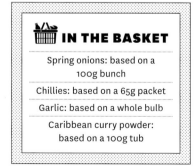

IN THE BASKET

Spring onions: based on a 100g bunch

Chillies: based on a 65g packet

Garlic: based on a whole bulb

Caribbean curry powder: based on a 100g tub

Chunky Sausage and Aubergine Stew

This is one of the simplest, tastiest stews you'll ever make. It's perfect for when you've just got home in the middle of winter and you want something properly filling and wholesome. It's incredibly satisfying and you can throw it together in 20 minutes.

Ingredients

1 tbsp olive oil
8 pork sausages
1 onion, finely chopped
1 aubergine, cut into 2cm chunks
4 garlic cloves, minced
400g tin chopped tomatoes
400g tin cannellini or butter beans
300ml beef stock, from a cube
4 slices crusty bread, toasted, to serve (optional)
salt and black pepper

Method

1. Put a pan on a high heat and pour in the oil, then add the sausages. Colour them all over and turn them regularly. This will take about 4 minutes. Take them out of the pan and set them aside.

2. Lower the heat under the pan to medium and add the onion and aubergine along with a pinch of salt. Let them cook for 3–4 minutes until they begin to soften. Add the minced garlic and cook for a further minute.

3. Tip in the tomatoes, beans and stock and add the sausages back in. Give everything a stir, put on the lid and simmer for 10 minutes.

4. Taste and add salt and black pepper to taste. Serve with the toasted crusty bread, if using.

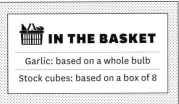

IN THE BASKET

Garlic: based on a whole bulb

Stock cubes: based on a box of 8

Honey Mustard Pork Chops and Vegetables

Pork chops are a cheap cut of meat that you can cook super-fast. At the time of writing this recipe, I bought four pork chops from a supermarket for just £2. Honey and mustard work well with pork chops; they go beautifully sticky and delicious. I finish off the vegetables in the same pan to soak up all the flavour! This is a real treat. Choose a cheaper supermarket brand of honey and buy the potatoes and carrots separately to save even more money.

Ingredients

6 carrots, cut into 2cm cubes

3 baking potatoes, skin on, cut into 2cm cubes

4 pork chops

1 tbsp vegetable or olive oil

150g honey

2 heaped tbsp wholegrain mustard

handful of fresh parsley, finely chopped (optional)

salt and black pepper

Method

1. Put the carrots and potatoes into a pan of cold salted water and bring them to a boil gradually. Cook them for 5–6 minutes. When they are fork tender, drain them and let them steam dry.

2. While the veggies are drying, season the chops on both sides with salt and black pepper. Put a pan on a high heat and add the oil, then lay the chops in the pan. You need to cook a 2.5cm-thick chop for 4 minutes on each side. This allows them to develop a nice brown crust on both sides.

3. While the chops are cooking, mix together the honey, mustard and a pinch of salt and black pepper in a small bowl. Pour the mixture over the chops, allow it to thicken in the pan for a minute and then baste the chops in the sauce. Take the chops out of the pan and set them aside.

4. Put the carrots and potatoes into the pan and allow them to soak up the honey mustard and pork flavours. Cook them for 1 minute, then place the chops next to the veggies.

5. Serve with the parsley, if using.

IN THE BASKET

Honey: based on a 340g jar

Wholegrain mustard: based on a 180g jar

Sharing and Picking Food

122

138

Paneer Kebabs with Garlic and Coriander Flatbreads

It's amazing how far you can stretch a fiver when you put your mind to it. This is a great example of taking the most humble ingredients and creating something really special! There are flavours here that will amaze you! You'll need to do a bit of multitasking to bring this one together fast, but have faith – you can do it!

Ingredients

1 green pepper, cut into 2cm chunks
2 red onions, cut into 2 cm chunks
2 tomatoes, quartered
225g paneer, cut into 2cm cubes
2 tbsp vegetable oil
2 tbsp curry powder
300g self-raising flour
2 garlic cloves, minced
15g fresh coriander, finely chopped, plus extra to serve
300g plain yoghurt, plus extra to serve
salt and black pepper

🗑 IN THE BASKET

Curry powder: based on an 85g tub

Flour: based on a 500g bag

Coriander: based on a 30g packet

Garlic: based on a whole bulb

Yoghurt: based on a 500ml tub

Method

1. Mix the pepper, onions, tomatoes and paneer in a large mixing bowl. Add the oil, curry powder and salt and pepper and mix everything together well.

2. Start to put everything on skewers; you can put the pieces on in any order you like but my preference is for tomato, onion, pepper and paneer repeated. Finish the skewer with a piece of tomato – makes them look pretty! You will fill 4 or 5 skewers with these quantities. Set them aside.

3. Put the flour, garlic, coriander and yoghurt in another bowl. Mix everything together until a dough starts to form. Flour a board and knead the dough on it for 2 minutes, then divide it into 4 or 5 equal pieces, depending on how many skewers you have.

4. Roll each piece of dough flat, put a pan on a high heat and cook the flatbreads one at a time for 1 minute on each side. You're want black char marks on both sides.

5. While the bread is cooking, put a dry griddle pan on a high heat and put the skewers on it. Cook them for 1 minute on each side, making sure that they are cooked on all 4 sides and that the paneer and vegetables are nicely charred.

6. When the skewers and bread are cooked, bring everything together on a serving board. I build my plate as follows: flatbread, yoghurt, skewered veggies and paneer, followed by a sprinkling of coriander.

Loaded Mixed Bean Chilli Nachos

One of the best combinations in food history has to be chilli and cheese. It hits the right spot for me. It's vegetarian to keep costs down and includes a tin of mixed beans to bulk it out. If your budget can stretch to minced beef that's also fine. You can also make your own chilli seasoning (see page 62).This is perfect sharing food, but there's also no shame in eating the lot yourself!

Ingredients

2 tbsp vegetable oil

1 onion, diced

1 yellow pepper, diced

4 garlic cloves, minced

41g packet chilli con carne seasoning

400g tin chopped tomatoes

400g tin mixed beans, drained

100ml water

10g fresh coriander, plus extra to serve

200g packet nachos or tortilla chips

125g ball mozzarella

Method

1. Put a pan on a medium heat and add the oil, onion and pepper. Let them cook for 5 minutes until they are soft. Add the garlic and cook for a further minute.
2. Tip in the chilli con carne seasoning and cook for 30 seconds. If everything seems too dry and the spices are starting to stick to the bottom of the pan, add a drop of water.
3. Add the tomatoes and beans along with the water. Give everything a good stir and let it bubble away on a low heat for 5 minutes. Stir through the coriander.
4. Take a baking dish and start to layer up the nachos and chilli. Start with a layer of nachos, followed by some of the chilli and continue in that pattern until you have used everything.
5. Break up the ball of mozzarella and spread it across the top.
6. Heat the grill to high, then put the baking tray under for 3–4 minutes until the cheese has melted and become golden. Serve with more finely chopped coriander.

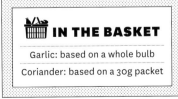

IN THE BASKET

Garlic: based on a whole bulb

Coriander: based on a 30g packet

Sausage Rolls with Honey Mustard Dip

This is a great addition to a party or buffet – these little beauties will impress your guests, I promise! Even if you're not throwing a party, they're a super snack to make with the kids or even just to treat yourself if you're feeling a little indulgent. I recommend buying your favourite sausages for these. I like a Cumberland sausage, but choose whichever one takes your fancy. Buy a sausage that you like!

Ingredients

6 pork sausages (I like Cumberland)
375g pack puff pastry sheets
1 egg, beaten
sprinkling of sesame seeds, to decorate (optional)
2 tbsp Dijon mustard
1 tbsp honey
juice of ½ lemon
salt and black pepper

Method

1. Preheat the oven to 200°C/180 C fan/gas mark 6.
2. Take the sausage meat out of the skins. Carefully score down the length of a sausage with a sharp knife and peel away the skin. With a bit of practice, it comes off in one piece!
3. Roll out the puff pastry and cut it in half lengthways. Put the sausage meat down the whole length and in the centre of the pastry (meat from 3 sausages per piece of pastry). Brush the edges of the pastry around the sausage meat with the beaten egg.
4. Fold the pastry over the top of the sausage meat on both sides. Trim off any excess pastry. You should have a tube of pastry with sausage meat in the middle, or an extra long sausage roll.
5. Brush the top of the sausage rolls with more beaten egg and then cut them into 2.5cm pieces to make small sausage rolls.
6. Top them with sesame seeds (if using) and put them into the oven for 20 minutes until they are golden brown.
7. Make the honey mustard dipping sauce by combining the mustard, honey, lemon juice and a pinch of salt and black pepper in a bowl. Mix them together until they are smooth and combined.

IN THE BASKET

Eggs: based on a box of 6

Dijon mustard: based on a 200g jar

Honey: based on a 200g jar

Salt and Pepper Cauliflower

This is similar to salt and pepper chicken but replaces the chicken with cauliflower. It's a great vegetarian alternative and you're going to love it. It is salty, garlicky, crunchy and spicy and a real treat, so give it a go! I use a deep-fat fryer for this recipe, but if you don't have one you can heat some vegetable oil in a pot and check the temperature using a thermometer. Make sure you chop all your vegetables before you start as everything cooks super fast!

Ingredients

500g plain flour
3 tsp Chinese five-spice seasoning
200ml cold water
1 cauliflower, leaves removed and
    broken into even-sized florets
    (about 4cm)
750ml vegetable oil, for deep
    frying, plus 3 tbsp to fry the
    peppers
1 onion, cut into 2cm chunks
2 peppers (1 red, 1 yellow), cut into
    2cm chunks
2 red chillies, roughly sliced
6 garlic cloves, finely chopped
5 spring onions, cut into
    2cm pieces
salt and black pepper

🗑 **IN THE BASKET**

Chinese five-spice: based
on a 40g jar

Chillies: based on a 65g packet

Garlic: based on a whole bulb

Spring onions: based on
a 100g bunch

Method

1. Divide the flour equally between 2 bowls. Add 1 teaspoon of Chinese five-spice and 1 each of salt and pepper to each bowl. Mix well, ensuring that everything is combined.

2. Slowly add the water to one of the bowls, stirring continuously to form a batter the consistency of paint.

3. Start coating the cauliflower: put a floret into the seasoned flour, then dunk it in the batter and then dip it into the flour again. Give it a generous coating so it will be nice and crispy! Repeat until all the florets are coated.

4. Heat a deep-fat fryer to 180°C and deep fry the florets for 3–4 minutes until the batter is golden brown and crispy. Take them out and set them aside.

5. Put a wok or a large sloping-sided pan on a high heat until it is screaming hot. Pour in the 3 tablespoons of oil, then add the onion, peppers and chillies and toss them for 1 minute until they slightly soften.

6. Add the garlic and continue to toss for a further minute, then the crispy florets and toss for 30 seconds.

7. Add the final teaspoon of Chinese five-spice along with salt and pepper (I recommend being generous with the salt to give you that authentic takeaway saltiness). Give everything a mix, add the spring onions and toss for a final 30 seconds.

8. Serve with the sliced red chillies, if using.

Spicy Peri Peri Wings

If you're a wuss when it comes to heat, approach these wings with caution. They have a serious kick! But if you're a spice lover, I've every confidence that you'll handle the heat. These wings are a fraction of the cost of wings from Nandos, so they have to be a winner! For the best results, I recommend grilling them on a BBQ for an authentic flavour. But you can oven bake them or even chuck them in an air fryer. For extra flavour, you can marinate the wings overnight.

Ingredients

1kg chicken wings
4 tbsp peri peri seasoning
4 large red chillies,
　roughly chopped
4 red birdseye chillies,
　roughly chopped
juice of 1 lemon
6 tbsp olive oil
handful of fresh coriander, finely
　chopped, to serve (optional)
salt and black pepper

Method

1.　If you cut the wings into 2 pieces (called the drumette and the wingette), you will end up with more pieces of chicken, which is a great way of stretching the wings to feed more people. Alternatively, leave them as they are. Put them in a mixing bowl and season with 3 tablespoons of peri peri seasoning and salt and pepper.

2.　Put all the chillies, 1 tablespoon of peri peri seasoning, the lemon juice, oil and salt and pepper in a food processor. Blitz them until smooth. Add a drop more oil If you like the sauce a little looser.

3.　Reserve half the sauce for later and pour the other half over the wings. Massage it into the wings. At this point you can leave them to marinate if you have time.

4.　If you are cooking on a barbecue, make sure it's very hot before putting on the wings. Cook them for 10–12 minutes, turning them every 2 minutes until they develop a nice black char all over. If you are baking them in an oven, preheat the oven to 180°C/160°C fan/gas mark 4, then put the wings on a baking tray and cook them for 20 minutes. Take them out and turn them over and then bake them for a further 20 minutes.

5.　When the wings are cooked through, brush on the remaining half of the sauce to finish them. Plate up and serve with the coriander, if using.

IN THE BASKET

Peri peri seasoning: based on a 40g jar
Chillies: based on a 65g packet
Birdseye chillies: based on a 20g packet

Pizza Turnovers

When I make these I rarely get the chance to eat one myself because my kids demolish them! If you have younger kids as I do, involve them in making these. They're fun and simple to make and the beauty of them is that you can top them with your favourite pizza toppings. I choose pepperoni and jalapeño slices – the world's your oyster though, so add whatever you like!

MAKES 12 TURNOVERS

Ingredients

2 x 375g packs puff pastry sheets
75g tomato purée
2 x 125g balls mozzarella
125g pack pepperoni, sliced
50g pickled jalapeños, finely chopped
1 egg, beaten (or you can use vegetable oil)
salt and black pepper

Method

1. Preheat the oven to 180°C/160°C fan/gas mark 4. Roll out the sheets of puff pastry and cut each sheet into six equal squares.
2. Put the tomato purée with some salt and pepper in a small bowl, plus a drop of water to loosen the sauce. Spread the mixture evenly over each square of pastry.
3. Break up the balls of mozzarella and divide them among the squares.
4. Top the squares with the pizza toppings of your choice. I add pepperoni slices and chopped pickled jalapeños.
5. Fold two opposite corners of each pastry square into the centre to make turnovers.
6. Brush each turnover with beaten egg and bake them for 15–20 minutes, or until they are golden brown.

IN THE BASKET

Tomato purée: based on a 200g tube

Jalapeños: based on a 200g jar

Bombay Potatoes

This is the ultimate way of turning the humble potato into a showstopper! Some may consider this to be a side dish, but I often make a batch and eat it as a main course. This recipe will give you four solid portions and you're going to absolutely love it!

Ingredients

1kg baking potatoes, skin on, cut into 2cm chunks

2 tbsp vegetable oil

1 onion, thinly sliced

1 red chilli, finely chopped

1 garlic bulb, cloves finely chopped

thumb-size piece of root ginger, chopped

handful of fresh coriander, finely chopped

2 tomatoes, each cut into 8 slices

3 tbsp curry powder (I use tandoori curry powder)

salt and black pepper

Method

1. Put the potato pieces into a saucepan, cover them with cold water and bring them to a simmer. Cook them for 10 minutes or until just tender. Drain them and set them aside.

2. Put a pan on a medium heat and add the oil and onion along with a pinch of salt. Fry the onion for 5 minutes, then add the chilli, garlic, ginger, the stalks of the coriander and the tomatoes and continue to cook for 2–3 minutes.

3. Add the curry powder and mix through for 30 seconds. Add a little water (2–3 tablespoons) to stop the spices sticking to the bottom of the pan and burning.

4. Add the cooked potatoes to the pan along with a generous pinch of salt. Move the potatoes around the pan to combine everything and allow them to absorb all the flavours.

5. Sprinkle with the coriander leaves and serve.

IN THE BASKET

Chillies: based on a 65g packet

Coriander: based on a 30g packet

Curry powder: based on an 85g tub

American-style Corn Dogs

I have no idea why we don't have food like this in the UK – these corn dogs are such a treat and incredibly cheap to make too. The dry ingredients in this recipe will allow you to make it three times over. All you'll need to buy the second and third time are more hot dogs and milk. Top them with any sauce that takes your fancy (I like ketchup and American mustard) and you have an absolute winner.

MAKES 5 CORN DOGS

Ingredients

150g self-raising flour
150g cornmeal
2 tsp granulated sugar
½ tsp salt
½ tsp black pepper
250ml milk
5 frankfurter hot dogs, from a jar
750ml vegetable oil, for
    deep frying
ketchup and American mustard,
    to serve

Method

1. Combine the flour, cornmeal, sugar, salt and pepper in a mixing bowl. Add the milk to the dry ingredients gradually, stirring continuously to form quite a thick batter. Pour the batter into a tall glass to make it easier to coat the hot dogs.

2. Push some wooden skewers lengthways through the hot dogs until they almost come out of the other end.

3. Set a deep-fat fryer to 180°C or heat some oil in a pot and check the temperature with a thermometer. Dunk a hot dog in the batter and completely submerge it. Gently rotate it to ensure that it is completely covered with batter. Then carefully and quickly drop the coated hot dog into the hot oil and fry it for 3 minutes (or until it is golden brown all over).

4. Repeat with the remaining hot dogs, then drain them on a piece of kitchen paper to soak up any excess oil.

5. Drizzle over some ketchup and American mustard to serve.

🗑 IN THE BASKET

Flour: based on a 500g bag

Cornmeal: based on a 500g bag

Sugar: based on a 1kg bag

Milk: based on a 1 pint bottle

Crispy Buffalo Chicken Wings

These are super tasty, budget buffalo chicken wings. Wings are the cheapest cut of chicken you can buy. At the time of writing, I bought 1kg of wings from a supermarket for £2.19 – incredible value for money! I'm a huge fan of hot sauce, so these wings always go down a treat. I've based the recipe on using Frank's RedHot Sauce, but you can use your favourite sauce and tweak the recipe however you want. It would work well with a good quality BBQ sauce too!

Ingredients

1kg chicken wings
500g plain flour
148ml bottle Frank's RedHot Sauce
2 tsp cayenne
200ml cold water
750ml vegetable oil, for
    deep frying
3 spring onions, finely chopped
    at an angle
salt and black pepper

Method

1. If you cut the wings into two pieces (called the drumette and the wingette) you will end up with more pieces of chicken, which is a great way of stretching the wings to feed more people. So separate the two parts if you like. Alternatively, you can leave them as they are.

2. Divide the flour between 2 bowls (put 300g in one and 200g in the other). Season each bowl with salt, pepper and a teaspoon of cayenne.

3. Slowly pour the water into the 200g flour bowl, mixing constantly. Keep mixing until the batter is smooth and free of lumps.

4. Put the wings into the flour first, shake off any excess, then dip them into the batter and finally put them into the flour again. Repeat this until all the wings are generously coated all over.

5. Set a deep-fat fryer to 170°C or heat some oil in a pot and use a thermometer to check the temperature. Deep fry the wings for 10–12 minutes until golden and crispy.

6. Put the cooked wings in a bowl, season with salt and pour over the whole bottle of hot sauce. Toss them in the bowl to coat all the wings in the sauce.

7. Plate up and serve with the spring onion.

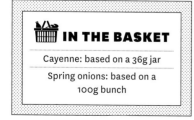

IN THE BASKET

Cayenne: based on a 36g jar

Spring onions: based on a 100g bunch

Crispy Parmesan and Garlic Potatoes

This is such an indulgent and moreish potato dish, which you can make with only four ingredients. It's perfect to put in the middle of the table so everyone can get stuck in. The quickest way to cook these is to deep fry them. They will taste just as good oven baked, but deep frying is much quicker!

Ingredients

1kg Maris Piper potatoes, skin on, cut into 2cm chunks
750ml vegetable oil, for deep frying, plus 1 tbsp vegetable or olive oil
4 garlic cloves, minced
80g Parmesan, grated
10g fresh chives, finely chopped, plus extra to serve
salt and black pepper

Method

1. Put the potatoes into a pan of cold water and bring them to a boil. Cook them for 7–8 minutes until they are fork tender. Drain them and let them sit for 5 minutes.

2. Heat a deep-fat fryer to 160°C or heat some oil in a pot and use a thermometer to check the temperature. Deep fry the potatoes for 4 minutes, then take them out and turn up the fryer to 190°C. Fry them for a further minute. This will give you very crispy and golden potatoes with soft and fluffy middles.

3. Pour a tablespoon of oil into a pan over a low heat pan, add the garlic and cook it for 2 minutes. Then add the crispy potatoes and toss them in the garlic.

4. Add the Parmesan and chives and toss everything together. Taste and add salt and black pepper if needed. Serve scattered with the chives.

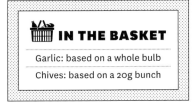

IN THE BASKET

Garlic: based on a whole bulb

Chives: based on a 20g bunch

Cheesy Chorizo Stuffed Mushrooms

Two of my favourite foods are combined in this recipe – chorizo and cheese. These mushrooms could be the most indulgent and moreish mushrooms you'll ever eat. I get cravings for them quite often, so it's fitting that I assign a warning to this recipe: you could become addicted to them!

AS A SIDE

Ingredients

200g cream cheese or soft cheese

70g pack thinly sliced chorizo, cut into 1cm pieces

3 spring onions (green parts only), thinly sliced, plus extra to serve

2 x 125g balls mozzarella, broken into small pieces

4 large flat white mushrooms, stalks removed

black pepper

Method

1. Preheat the oven to 200°C/180°C fan/gas mark 6.
2. Put the cheese, chorizo, spring onions, one mozzarella ball and a crack of black pepper in a bowl. Mix them together until everything is nicely combined and smooth.
3. Put the mushroom tops on a baking tray and divide the mixture equally among them.
4. Top with the second ball of mozzarella, spreading it over the mushrooms equally.
5. Put the baking tray into the oven and cook for 20 minutes, or until the mozzarella on top has gone beautifully golden.
6. Serve with sliced spring onions.

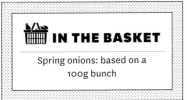

IN THE BASKET

Spring onions: based on a 100g bunch

Crispy Curried Fish Tacos

You need to be in the zone to cook this one – there's a lot to do so you have to be ready to dash around the kitchen and multitask to make the ultimate family feast! You can find some great bargains in the frozen food sections of supermarkets: at the time of writing, I bought 500g of fish fillets for £2.50 for this recipe and had plenty to serve four people! Just ensure that you move frozen fish from the freezer to the fridge the day before cooking to defrost. The list of ingredients seems long but many of them can be used in other recipes. If you want to save time you can buy ready-made tortillas. I prefer to make my own because it's cheaper and I like them quite rustic.

Ingredients

For the fish
500g frozen fish fillets, cut into 2cm chunks (recipe is based on using pollock)
200g plain yoghurt, plus extra to serve
4 tbsp curry powder
juice of ½ lemon
200g plain flour
750ml vegetable oil, for deep frying
salt and black pepper

For the tortillas
250g plain flour
½ tsp salt
1 tbsp olive oil
130ml cold tap water

Method

1. Put the fish pieces into a bowl. Add the yoghurt, 2 tablespoons of curry powder, the lemon juice and salt and pepper to taste. Give everything a good mix and set the bowl aside while you make the dough for the tortillas.

2. To make the tortillas, put the flour, salt, oil and water into a bowl. Bring them together with your hands until they begin to form a dough.

3. Flour a board, put the dough on it and knead it for a couple of minutes. If it seems wet you can add a little more flour. Divide the dough into 4 pieces and roll them to the thickness of a £1 coin.

4. If you want all your tortillas the same size, use a cereal bowl and cut round it. You should be able to make 10 tortillas from these quantities.

5. Heat a pan until it's screaming hot and put the tortillas in one at a time. They will cook in about 30 seconds on each side and you want some black char marks. Repeat until they are all cooked.

6. Mix the salad ingredients with the lemon juice, oil and salt and pepper to taste.

7. Return to the fish and put the flour, the remaining 2 tablespoons of curry powder and salt and pepper into a bowl. Take a few pieces of the fish at a time and dredge them in the flour until they are generously coated. Repeat until all the fish is coated.

For the salad

½ red chilli, finely diced, plus
    extra slices to serve
1 red onion, finely diced
1 tomato, finely diced
juice of ½ lemon
1 tbsp olive oil
small handful of fresh coriander,
    plus extra to serve (optional)
salt and black pepper

8. Heat a deep-fat fryer to 180°C or heat some oil in a pot and use a
    thermometer to check the temperature. Cook the fish pieces for
    3 minutes until they are golden.
9. Put everything on a serving board and let everyone dig in. I assemble
    the tortillas as follows: take a tortilla, add a tablespoon of yoghurt
    then one of salad, followed by a few pieces of crispy fish and then
    decorate with some chilli slices and coriander, if using.

🧺 IN THE BASKET

Yoghurt: based on a 500ml tub

Curry powder: based on an
85g tub

Flour: based on a 500g bag

Chillies: based on a 65g packet

Cajun Pork Kebabs

This is a great little recipe for when you fancy dusting off the barbecue and enjoying a sunny day. But if it's raining you can cook them just as easily on a griddle pan in the comfort of your own kitchen! I recommend using a barbecue if possible, because flame grilling raises the flavour to a different level. I have based this recipe on using cheap pork loin steaks as this is a great way of elevating a budget cut of meat into a real treat. It really is simple – just cut up the pork, peppers and onion, skewer them and grill them.

Ingredients

4 pork loin steaks, cut into
   3cm chunks
1 red pepper, cut into 3cm chunks
1 green pepper, cut into
   3cm chunks
1 red onion, cut into 3cm chunks
2 tbsp Cajun seasoning
2 tbsp olive oil
salt and black pepper

Method

1. Combine the pork pieces, peppers, onion, Cajun seasoning, oil and some salt and black pepper in a large bowl. Mix everything together and don't be afraid to use your hands to massage the seasoning into the meat and veggies.

2. Take 4 skewers; if they're wooden, soak them in cold water for at least 30 minutes so they won't catch fire on the barbecue. Thread the pork and veggies on to the skewers. I like a pattern of pepper, pork, onion and repeat – makes them pleasing on the eye! Divide the pork and veggies evenly among the 4 skewers.

3. Heat the barbecue or an outdoor grill to a high heat and put on the skewers. Cook them for 10–12 minutes, turning them every 2 minutes. You want a nice black char, with the kebabs close to burning.

4. When the kebabs are cooked through, serve them piping hot.

IN THE BASKET

Cajun seasoning: based on a
47g jar

Quick Halloumi and Guacamole Pittas

There is something special about halloumi – I love it and it seems to go with everything. It may not be long before people start to put it on ice cream or even their Sunday roast! These quick pittas are great for a speedy lunch when you are busy. Simply grill the halloumi, chop your fresh stuff and bring it all together. So simple and it tastes great.

Ingredients

2 avocados, stoned
1 tomato, finely diced
½ green chilli, deseeded and
    finely diced, plus slices to serve
½ red onion, finely diced
juice of ½ a lime
handful of fresh coriander, finely
    chopped, plus extra to serve
3 tbsp olive oil
225g halloumi, cut into batons
4 pittas
salt and black pepper

Method

1. Put the avocados, tomato, chilli, onion, lime juice, coriander, 2 tablespoons of oil, salt and black pepper into a bowl. Use a fork to mash the avocado and mix together, ensuring that everything is well combined.

2. Put a griddle pan on a high heat and add 1 tablespoon of oil to prevent the halloumi sticking. Cook the halloumi for 30 seconds on each side, or until it's coloured to your liking.

3. Microwave the pittas for 30 seconds then assemble them as follows: take a couple of tablespoons of guacamole, then add some halloumi batons, and top with some coriander and sliced chilli.

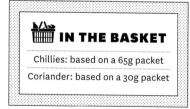

IN THE BASKET

Chillies: based on a 65g packet

Coriander: based on a 30g packet

My Ultimate Potato Salad

If you're bored with standard potato salad, then here's a great little recipe that elevates it to another level. You're going to be surprised how good this tastes despite being made with just a few simple ingredients. You'll never go back to boring shop-bought potato salad ever again!

Ingredients

700g new or baby potatoes, cut into 3cm pieces
300ml sour cream
juice of ½ lemon
2 tbsp olive oil
2 tbsp curry powder
½ red onion, thinly sliced, plus extra to serve
10g fresh coriander, finely chopped, plus extra to serve
salt and black pepper

Method

1. Put the potatoes into cold salted water and bring them to a boil. They will take 10–12 minutes to soften – you want them to be fork tender. Drain them and let them dry and cool. You can speed this up by putting them in the fridge.
2. Meanwhile, put the sour cream, lemon juice, oil, curry powder, onion, coriander and salt and black pepper in a bowl and mix them well.
3. When the potatoes have cooled, add them to the bowl and mix everything thoroughly.
4. Serve in the bowl with extra onion slices and coriander.

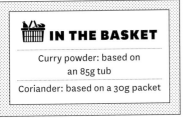

IN THE BASKET

Curry powder: based on an 85g tub

Coriander: based on a 30g packet

Leftovers

146

148

154

158

Peri Peri Fried Rice with Halloumi

This is another super-quick recipe that turns dull and bland leftover rice into something special. Halloumi just seems to make every dish better and is one of my favourite cheeses! You could probably throw this together in 10 minutes from start to finish. Enjoy it: it's properly tasty.

Ingredients

1 tbsp vegetable oil
1 yellow pepper, diced
1 red onion, diced
4 garlic cloves, minced
600g leftover cooked rice, chilled
25g peri peri seasoning
225g halloumi, cut into batons
a handful of fresh coriander, finely
    chopped, to serve (optional)
salt and black pepper

Method

1. Put a pan on a medium heat and add the oil, pepper and onion along with a pinch of salt. Let this cook for 2–3 minutes until it begins to slightly soften. Add the garlic and continue to cook for 1 minute.

2. Add the cooked rice along with the peri peri seasoning and mix everything together. Ensure that you break up the rice; you don't want big clumps. Try using the back of a ladle to break them up. Turn the heat down to the lowest setting to keep everything warm. Taste and add some salt and black pepper if necessary.

3. Heat a griddle pan on a high heat and grill the halloumi batons. You want them to have some black char marks. They will take about a minute and a half on each side (depending on how thick they are).

4. Put the cooked halloumi on top of the rice in the other pan and serve with the coriander, if using.

Crispy Potato Skins with Sour Cream and Chive Dip

Just think about the number of times you've peeled potatoes for mash and chucked all the peel in the bin! Well let me tell you now: stop doing that! Don't throw away potato peelings; they can be the best part of the spud when cooked right. This recipe is so simple and gives you a great little snack or side dish that goes down a treat! The skins pair beautifully with a homemade sour cream and chive dip, although you can happily dip them in anything you have in your fridge or cupboards!

Ingredients

leftover potato peelings from
    1kg potatoes
2 tbsp olive oil
½ tsp paprika
½ tsp garlic powder
½ tsp chilli flakes
salt and pepper

For the dip
2 heaped tbsp sour cream
2 heaped tbsp mayonnaise
a few fresh chives, finely chopped,
    plus extra to serve
1 garlic clove, minced
juice of ½ lemon
pinch of salt

Method

1. Preheat the oven to 190°C/170°C fan/gas mark 5. Wash the potato peels in cold water and then pat them dry with a tea towel or kitchen paper.

2. Put them into a bowl and add the oil, spices and seasoning. Mix well to ensure that all the peels are well seasoned.

3. Place them on a baking tray – don't overcrowd it and spread the peels across 2 trays if necessary. Bake in the oven for 20 minutes or until they are beautifully crispy.

4. Make the dip by combining all the ingredients in a bowl and stirring well.

5. Place the dip in the centre of a large plate and scatter the crispy peels around it, sprinkled with some more chives.

Vegetable Pakoras

The chances are that you'll have carrots and potatoes in your fridge on the verge of going to waste at some point. So why not have a crack at these vegetable pakoras? If you're not sure what they are, they're very similar to onion bhajis, except they include veggies such as carrots and potatoes. Pakoras are deep-fried bites of happiness and can be made in no time at all! Traditionally you use gram (chickpea) flour to make the batter, but if you can't find any then use plain flour.

Ingredients

3 baking potatoes, peeled and thinly sliced, then cut into matchsticks
1 carrot, grated
1 onion, thinly sliced
10g fresh coriander, finely chopped, plus extra to serve
1 red chilli, finely chopped
thumb-size piece of ginger, finely chopped
5 garlic cloves, finely chopped
4 tbsp curry powder
200g gram or plain flour
130ml cold water
750ml vegetable oil, for deep frying
salt and black pepper

Method

1. Put the potato pieces, carrot, onion, coriander, chilli, ginger, garlic and curry powder in a large bowl and add salt and black pepper to taste. Mix everything together until well combined.
2. Tip in the flour and then gradually add the water, while continuing to mix. The mixture will become quite sticky and everything will start to clump together.
3. Set the deep-fat fryer to 180°C, or heat some vegetable oil in a pan and check the temperature with a thermometer. Take a heaped tablespoonful of the mixture and spoon it into the hot oil – each tablespoon of mixture will become a pakora. Deep fry them for 4–5 minutes until they are golden brown and crispy.
4. Serve sprinkled with coriander.

Veggie Fried Rice

In my house I often cook way too much rice. I have loads left over when I'm cooking a curry or chilli! I'm always coming up with different ways to use the leftovers so they don't go to waste. This veggie fried rice is a great budget-friendly way of doing just that. It's a meal on its own and so versatile too – you can mix and match all sorts of veggies and experiment to find which work best. I keep leftover rice in the fridge and make this recipe the following day – it always turns out best that way!

Ingredients

2 tbsp vegetable oil
1 onion, diced
1 carrot, diced
1 yellow pepper, diced
3 garlic cloves, minced
600g leftover cooked rice, chilled
3 medium eggs, beaten
100g frozen peas
5 tbsp dark soy sauce
5 spring onions (green parts only),
   finely chopped on an angle
salt

Method

1. Put a pan on a high heat and pour in the oil. Add the onion, carrot, pepper and a pinch of salt. Let it cook for 2 minutes. Add the garlic and continue to cook for 1 minute.

2. Add the cooked rice and break it up with the back of a ladle or a wooden spoon. You don't want any large clumps of rice.

3. Make a well in the centre of the pan and pour in the beaten eggs. Stir them into the rice for 1 minute.

4. Add the frozen peas and soy sauce and continue to cook for a further minute (or until the peas have thawed). The soy sauce will stain the rice a nice brown colour.

5. Put the fried rice into a bowl and compress it, then turn the bowl over on a plate to make a tasty-looking domed pile. Serve with the spring onions.

Greek-style Feta Pasta Salad

This really is a top tier salad. I'm not known for my salad recipes but sometimes on a warm day I need to eat something fresh and cooling like this – it does me the world of good! I always cook too much pasta and end up with loads left over. The beauty of this recipe is that you can use any pasta shape; the one I use most often is penne. You can even cut up leftover lasagne sheets – use whatever you have. You can also use different salad ingredients if you prefer. Just chuck everything into a large mixing bowl and serve.

Ingredients

300g leftover cooked penne (or other pasta)
1 yellow pepper, diced
½ cucumber, diced
200g cherry tomatoes, quartered
30g black olives, thinly sliced
70g baby salad leaves
200g feta or Greek salad cheese, cubed
juice of ½ lemon, plus a wedge to serve
3 tbsp olive oil, plus extra for drizzling
salt and black pepper

Method

1. Put the cooled pasta, pepper, cucumber, tomatoes, olives, salad leaves and feta into a large mixing bowl. Give everything a good mix – use your hands and mix with the tips of your fingers.
2. Pour in the lemon juice and oil along with salt and black pepper to taste. Give everything one final toss.
3. Serve with a lemon wedge and a drizzle of oil.

Black Bean and Rice Burritos

These are very simple burritos bulked out with leftover cooked rice. For this recipe I use a smoky chipotle seasoning blend, but a decent fajita or peri peri seasoning would work well too. Deseed the chilli if you're not keen on heat. These can be made from start to finish in 15 minutes!

Ingredients

1 tbsp vegetable oil
1 red onion, finely chopped
1 red chilli, finely chopped
1 yellow pepper, finely chopped
4 garlic cloves, finely chopped
2 tbsp smoky chipotle seasoning
400g tin chopped tomatoes
400g tin black beans, drained
600g leftover cooked rice, chilled
6 tortilla wraps (20cm diameter)
salt and black pepper

Method

1. Put a pan on a medium heat and add the oil, onion, chilli and pepper along with a pinch of salt. Cook for 3–4 minutes until the mixture begins to soften. Add the garlic and cook for a further minute, then the chipotle seasoning and cook for 30 seconds.

2. Tip in the tomatoes, beans and cooked rice. Mix everything together and cook it for 2 minutes to bring the rice up to temperature. Taste and season with salt and black pepper.

3. Divide the contents of the pan evenly among the tortillas, then wrap them up. The best way to do this is to put the rice mixture about 2.5cm from the tortilla edge closest to you, then fold in the sides and roll it away from you while tucking the edges in tightly. This can take practice – if you find it difficult, put less filling into each one until you build up confidence.

4. Put a griddle pan on a high heat, add the burritos and seal them for 30 seconds on each side. You want some nice black bar marks.

5. Slice the burritos in half on an angle and serve.

Pasta Crisps

I always cook too much pasta! When you're in a rush it's difficult to judge how much to put in the pan. This is a great way of using up leftover cooked pasta and turns it into something completely different. It's a great little snack that you'll love.

Ingredients

For the pasta
400g leftover cooked pasta
20g Parmesan, grated
1 tsp Italian seasoning
2 tbsp olive oil
salt and black pepper

For the sauce
400g tin tomatoes
20g Parmesan, grated
2 tsp Italian seasoning
10 fresh basil leaves, plus extra
    to serve
2 tbsp olive oil
salt and black pepper

Method

1. Preheat the oven to 200°C/180°C fan/gas mark 6. Put the cooked pasta, Parmesan, seasoning, olive oil and salt and black pepper into a bowl. Mix everything well and then put it on a baking tray and bake it for 20 minutes (or until it's crispy).

2. Meanwhile, put the sauce ingredients into a food processor and blitz until smooth. I prefer the sauce cold as it works well with the warm, crispy pasta. Transfer the sauce into a ramekin or bowl to serve.

3. Plate up the crispy pasta sauce and enjoy it with the sauce sprinkled with more fresh basil.

Leftovers Soup

One-pot soup made from leftovers is a meal based on
raiding your cupboards and fridge for anything you have and
chucking it together to make a quick budget soup. It's one of
those meals in which you use anything you have left the day
before your weekly food shop, so nothing goes to waste. You
can add whatever you like – it's about creating something
filling and cheap that sees you through!

Ingredients

4 slices bacon, chopped into
   1cm pieces
1 tbsp vegetable oil
1 onion, finely chopped
1 stick celery, finely chopped
3 garlic cloves, finely chopped
1 tsp dried mixed herbs
400g tin tomatoes
100g frozen mixed vegetables
   (peas, sweetcorn, carrots)
150g macaroni
1 chicken stock cube
salt and black pepper
handful of fresh parsley, finely
   chopped (optional)

Method

1. Put the bacon into a cold pan along with the oil and bring the heat
   gradually up to high. Cook the bacon for 3–4 minutes or until it is
   crispy, then take it out and set it aside.

2. Lower the heat under the pan to medium and add the onion and
   celery along with a pinch of salt and soften them for 3–4 minutes.
   Add the chopped garlic and mixed herbs and continue to cook for a
   further minute.

3. Add the tomatoes, mixed veg, macaroni and stock cube, then fill the
   empty tin with cold water twice and pour the water into the pan.
   Give everything a stir, then put the lid on the pan and simmer for
   15 minutes or until the pasta is cooked.

4. Taste and season with salt and black pepper. Serve with the parsley,
   if using.

Homemade Onion Rings with Cajun Mayo

If you have a couple of onions knocking about, then have a crack at this very simple recipe. They are crispy, indulgent and amazingly tasty. I've added a simple Cajun mayo recipe here, but you can pair them with any sauce you like! Or you can eat them on their own. If you want to elevate this even further, you could swap the sparkling water for some beer to make a homemade beer batter.

Ingredients

For the onion rings
750ml vegetable oil, for
    deep frying
200g plain flour
2 tbsp Cajun seasoning
2 onions, peeled and cut into 1cm
    thick rings
220ml sparkling water
salt and black pepper

For the Cajun mayo
3 heaped tbsp mayo
½ garlic clove, minced
½ tsp Cajun seasoning
1 tsp lemon juice
salt and black pepper

Method

1. Heat a deep-fat fryer to 180°C or heat some vegetable oil in a pot on the stove, monitoring the temperature with a cooking thermometer.
2. Put the flour, Cajun seasoning and salt and black pepper in a bowl and mix them together thoroughly.
3. Put the onion rings into the flour, coat them all over, and shake off any excess, then set them aside (this helps the batter to stick to the onion rings). Add the sparkling water to the flour bowl gradually, while whisking continuously. You want a batter with a smooth consistency and no lumps.
4. Coat the onion rings in the batter one by one and then carefully drop them into the hot oil. Don't overcrowd the pan and cook them in batches if necessary. Deep fry them for 4–5 minutes until they are beautifully golden and crispy.
5. Combine all the Cajun mayo ingredients in a ramekin or small bowl and mix them together well. Serve the mayo with the onion rings and add another pinch of Cajun seasoning to the top of the mayo to decorate.

Tuna Potato Cake Burgers

This is a great recipe if you have leftover potatoes in your fridge on the verge of being past their best, or if you've cooked too much mashed potato for your Sunday dinner. Don't let any go to waste! Give these tuna potato cake burgers a try and you'll be making them time and time again. I remember the first time I made these for my kids – they wolfed them down!

Ingredients

800g potatoes (about 4 baking
   potatoes), peeled and cut into
   2cm chunks
2 heaped tbsp plain flour
110g tin tuna
4 spring onions, finely sliced
2 tbsp olive or vegetable oil
4 seeded brioche buns
4 tbsp tartar sauce
½ iceberg lettuce, shredded
1 lemon, cut into wedges
   for squeezing
salt and black pepper

Method

1. Put the potatoes into cold salted water, bring them to the boil and cook them until they are soft and breaking apart, then drain. This will take about 10 minutes (skip this step if you are using leftover mashed potato).

2. Put the potatoes into a bowl and add the flour, the tuna and spring onions and season with salt and pepper. Mash everything together with a potato masher until it's all well combined.

3. Divide the mixture into 4 portions and roll them into balls. Gently press the balls flat until they are 2.5cm thick and smooth them with your hands into a burger shape.

4. Put a pan on a medium heat and add the oil, then carefully place the potato cakes in the pan and cook them for 2 minutes on each side until they are golden brown. Meanwhile, toast the buns.

5. Assemble the burgers: start with the toasted bottom half of a bun, spread on a tablespoon of tartar sauce, then add some lettuce followed by a potato cake, a squeeze of lemon juice and finally the top half of the bun.

Sweet
Stuff

166

170

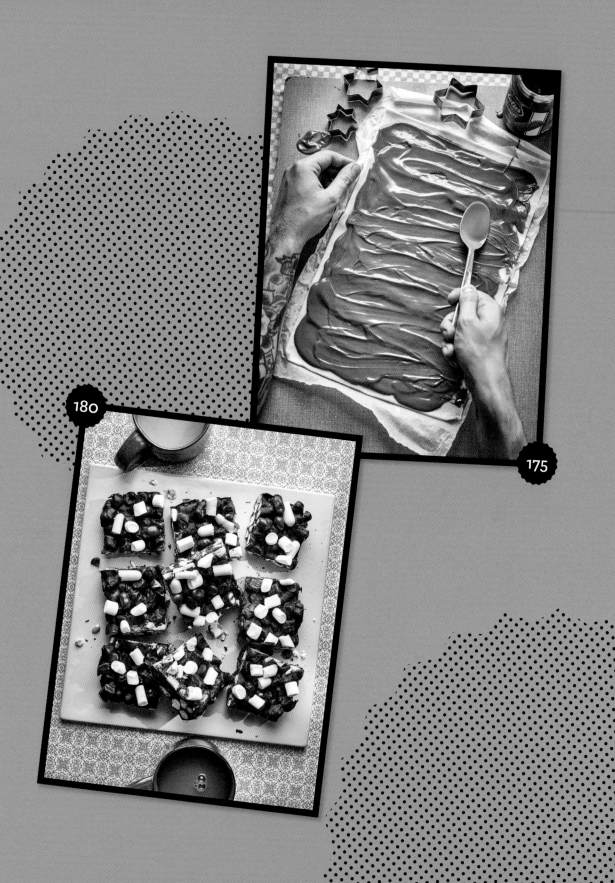

Oreo Truffles

You only need four ingredients to make these bite-sized chunks of pure sweetness. If you have a sweet tooth, or you crave something a little bit indulgent, this is perfection! You can crush the biscuits in a food processor or put them into a large mixing bowl and bash them with a rolling pin. This will make 16 truffle balls so there will be plenty to go round. Have a go – you won't be disappointed.

Ingredients

300g Oreos or supermarket own brand equivalent, crushed to fine crumbs
150g cream cheese or soft cheese
300g milk chocolate
50g white chocolate

Method

1. Put aside about 15g of the crushed biscuits for later.
2. Put the cheese and the biscuit crumbs into a large bowl and mix them until they are well combined.
3. Divide the mixture into 16 balls and roll them in your hands to make them smooth. Put them on a tray in the freezer for 8–10 minutes.
4. Melt the milk chocolate, either in 30-second bursts in the microwave or in a saucepan on the hob.
5. Dunk the biscuit balls in the chocolate and then freeze them again for a further 2 minutes.
6. Melt the white chocolate and drizzle it over the balls, then sprinkle them with the remaining 15g of crushed biscuits to decorate.

IN THE BASKET

Cream cheese: based on a 200g tub

White chocolate: based on a 100g bar

No-bake Crispy Cake

This is a five-ingredient dessert that's an absolute winner! It's one of those desserts that takes me back to school where I bought it by the square. It's very versatile and can be easily tweaked. You can swap the white chocolate buttons for any chocolate, or even melt the buttons and drizzle melted white chocolate over the top. This recipe would also work with cornflakes. Cut the squares as big or as small as you like – small ones if you're watching what you eat. Or eat the entire slab!

Ingredients

300g milk chocolate
100g marshmallows
100g butter or baking spread
160g Coco Pops cereal or
   supermarket own brand
   equivalent
70g white chocolate buttons

Method

1. Put a saucepan on a low heat and add 100g of the milk chocolate, the marshmallows and the butter. Stir continuously for 3–4 minutes until everything has melted and combined.
2. Add the cereal and mix it through thoroughly, ensuring it's all coated in the chocolate and marshmallow mixture.
3. Transfer the mixture to a 25 x 18cm lined baking tray and press it down with the back of a spoon so it's nice and compact.
4. Melt the remaining 200g of milk chocolate in the microwave in 30-second bursts until smooth.
5. Pour the melted chocolate over the top of the cake and spread it out evenly with the back of a spoon.
6. Top the cake with the buttons. Make it as messy or as neat as you like! Put it in the freezer for 10 minutes.
7. Remove the cake from the baking tray and cut it into squares.

🛒 IN THE BASKET

Marshmallows: based on a 180g bag

Butter: based on a 500g block

Cereal: based on a 295g box

Chocolate Cheesecake Cups

If you're like me and love cheesecake but don't want to spend hours making it, this is for you. These cheesecake cups taste amazing but you won't be stuck in the kitchen for an eternity while making them! You'll need some small glasses to make these in so everyone can have their own individual cheesecake. I use glasses 12cm tall and 8cm wide. These quantities will make six portions; but you could swap the glasses for ramekins or whatever you have in your kitchen cupboards.

Ingredients

200g Bourbon biscuits or own
  brand equivalent
300g milk chocolate
300g soft cheese or cream cheese
50g icing sugar
300ml double cream

Method

1. Blitz the biscuits in a food processor until you have very fine crumbs.
2. Melt 100g of the chocolate in a pan on a low heat or in a microwave in 30-second bursts. Combine the chocolate and biscuits and divide the mixture equally among the 6 glasses. Press it down into the bottom of the glasses with the back of a spoon so it's nicely compact. Put the glasses into the fridge to chill.
3. Meanwhile, melt 180g of the chocolate and allow it to cool slightly to room temperature. Mix the soft cheese and icing sugar until they are well combined, then pour in the melted chocolate and mix again.
4. Whisk 150ml of the double cream in another bowl until it stands in stiff peaks and then fold the cream into the cheese and icing sugar mixture.
5. Use a piping bag if you have one to pipe the mixture into the glasses on top of the crushed biscuits. Divide it equally among the 6 glasses. If you don't have a piping bag, spoon it into the glasses. Return the glasses to the fridge to chill.
6. Whisk the remaining 150ml of cream until it stands in stiff peaks and then top the glasses with it.
7. Grate the remaining 20g of chocolate on top of the cream to decorate. Chill the glasses in the fridge for about 10 minutes before serving.

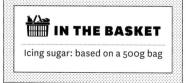

IN THE BASKET

Icing sugar: based on a 500g bag

Muesli Bars

Yes, you need just three ingredients to make these little beauties! They're super chewy, really moreish and much cheaper than store-bought bars. I use muesli containing dried fruit and nuts from the cereal section in the supermarket. Choose any you like – you can add extra dried fruit and nuts if you prefer.

Ingredients

500g muesli
397g tin condensed milk
100g white chocolate

Method

1. Preheat the oven to 180°C/160°C fan/gas mark Combine the muesli and condensed milk in a large mixing bowl and mix thoroughly so there are no dry bits of muesli.
2. Grease and line a 25 x 15cm baking tray with baking paper. Tip in the muesli mixture and spread it out evenly. Press it down with the back of a spoon to compress it.
3. Bake on the middle shelf of the oven for 15 minutes.
4. Allow the mixture to cool for 10 minutes and then cut it into bars. Melt the chocolate in the microwave and drizzle it over the bars. Serve and enjoy.

Nutella and Kinder Turnovers

This is a simple and speedy little recipe that I love making with my kids. You can eat these turnovers hot or let them cool and save them for later. I use a budget supermarket own brand version of Nutella for this to keep costs down. I also add a few squares of Kinder chocolate to make them extra indulgent. You're not likely to lose weight eating them – so treat yourself.

Ingredients

375g sheet ready-made shortcrust pastry
6 tbsp Nutella or own brand supermarket spread
60g Kinder chocolate, broken into pieces
1 egg, beaten (or use vegetable oil)
icing sugar, to dust

Method

1. Preheat the oven to 180°C/160°C fan/gas mark 4. Divide the pastry into 6 equal squares – you may need to use a ruler to make them as similar as possible.
2. Put a tablespoon of the spread on each square and spread it out, then top with 10g of Kinder chocolate.
3. Carefully fold 2 opposite corners into the centre of a square and press the corners together gently to create a turnover shape. Repeat with the remaining squares.
4. Brush each turnover with the beaten egg to help them turn golden in the oven.
5. Put the turnovers on a baking tray and bake them for 15 minutes.
6. Sieve over a light dusting of icing sugar to finish the turnovers.

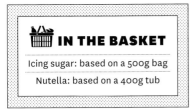

IN THE BASKET

Icing sugar: based on a 500g bag

Nutella: based on a 400g tub

Shortcrust Stars

These have just three ingredients – they couldn't be any simpler! I've used a star-shaped cookie cutter for this recipe, but you could use anything you have. You can make different shapes for festive occasions (Christmas trees, pumpkins for Halloween, and so on). The same applies to the filling. I use a supermarket own brand version of Biscoff spread, but you could also use Nutella. Make them the way you like them!

Ingredients

400g Biscoff or own brand
  supermarket biscuit spread
2 x 375g ready-made shortcrust
  pastry sheets
icing sugar, to dust

Method

1. Preheat the oven to 180°C/160°C fan/gas mark 4. Microwave the jar of spread for 30 seconds until it has a spreadable caramel consistency.
2. Put one of the sheets of pastry on a baking tray and pour the spread on to it. Spread it all over the pastry with the back of a spoon.
3. Lay the other sheet of pastry on top to sandwich the biscuit spread in the middle.
4. Use a star-shaped cookie cutter to cut out as many stars as you can.
5. Put the stars on a baking tray and bake them for 10–12 minutes, or until they start to go golden brown. Keep a close eye on them as they can burn very easily.
6. Sieve over a dusting of icing sugar and enjoy the stars when warm.

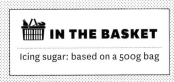

IN THE BASKET

Icing sugar: based on a 500g bag

Biscoff Dough Balls

I am drooling just thinking about these – made with only five ingredients! They are simple, quick and properly naughty. Basically, they're chocolate-stuffed dough balls coated in melted Biscoff spread and then rolled in crushed Biscoff biscuits. They are little balls of caramelized sweetness and I wouldn't have them any other way!

Ingredients

400g self-raising flour, plus extra for kneading

350g vanilla yoghurt

150g milk chocolate, broken into small pieces

400g Biscoff or supermarket own brand biscuit spread

750ml vegetable oil, for deep frying

250g Biscoff or supermarket own brand biscuits, blitzed into crumbs

Method

1. Combine the flour and yoghurt in a mixing bowl. Mix until they start to form a dough.

2. Flour a board and knead the dough for 2–3 minutes to bring it together. If it's a little sticky, add another dusting of flour.

3. Put 100g of the chocolate pieces into a bowl. Break off a piece of dough about the size of a golf ball and flatten it slightly in your hand. Take a small piece of chocolate, press it into the centre of the ball and fold the dough round the chocolate. This will give the dough ball an oozy chocolate centre. Repeat with the remaining dough and chocolate pieces.

4. Set a deep-fat fryer to 180°C or heat some vegetable oil in a pot and use a thermometer to check the temperature. Deep fry the dough balls in batches for 3–4 minutes until they are golden brown all over. Turn them regularly in the oil so they cook evenly. You'll notice they puff up in size.

5. Melt the Biscoff spread in the microwave for 30–45 seconds until it's smooth.

6. Roll the crispy dough balls one by one in the melted spread, ensuring that you coat them all over.

7. Then drop them into the crushed biscuits and roll them around to give them an even crust of crumbs. Repeat until they are all coated.

8. Pile them up on a plate and melt the remaining 50g of chocolate to drizzle over them. Enjoy them warm.

IN THE BASKET

Flour: based on a 500g bag

Yoghurt: based on a 500g tub

Chocolate Hazelnut Spread Traybake

I absolutely love a bit of cake! And this is probably the easiest cake recipe you'll ever see. It has just four ingredients and to keep the cost as low as possible, I use a supermarket own brand equivalent of Nutella. Then I just put everything in a bowl, whisk it up and put it in the oven

Ingredients

400g chocolate hazelnut spread
70g self-raising flour
3 medium eggs
50g white chocolate

Method

1. Preheat the oven to 180°C/160°C fan/gas mark 4. Grease and line a 25 x 15cm baking tray.
2. Combine the spread, flour and eggs in a mixing bowl. Whisk everything together until you have a smooth mixture.
3. Put the mixture into the baking tray and bake it on the middle shelf of the oven for 20 minutes. Check if it's cooked by piercing the middle of the cake with a skewer. If it comes out clean, it's ready.
4. Melt the chocolate in the microwave in 30-second bursts until it's smooth, then drizzle it over the cake. You can make it as pretty or messy as you like!
5. Cut it into squares and enjoy it hot or cold.

IN THE BASKET

Eggs: based on a box of 6

Flour: based on a 500g bag

White chocolate: based on a 100g bar

Rocky Road

This is probably the easiest rocky road recipe you'll ever lay your eyes on and you can make it from just four simple and easily accessible ingredients. But you can also make this recipe as complicated or extravagant as you like. The secret to a good rocky road is to have as many different textures as possible: crispy, crunchy, gooey and so on. This is my version and you're going to love it! I use dark chocolate because I think it works really well, but you could use milk or even white chocolate. For the gooey part I use marshmallows, the crispy part comes from chocolate peanuts and crunchy part from white chocolate finger biscuits. You could add some jelly sweets or even use shortbread biscuits instead of the fingers. Make it the way you like it!

Ingredients

400g dark chocolate

100g mini marshmallows, plus extra to decorate

100g chocolate coated peanuts, plus extra to decorate

100g white chocolate finger biscuits, broken into 1cm pieces, plus extra to decorate

Method

1. Put the chocolate in a bowl and melt it in the microwave on 30-second bursts until it's smooth. It should only take 2 minutes to melt.

2. Take the bowl out and add the marshmallows, peanuts and biscuits and mix everything thoroughly.

3. Line a 20 x 20cm baking tray with baking paper and transfer the mixture into it. Press down on it with the back of a spoon, to ensure it is compact and pushed into the corners of the tray.

4. Top with more marshmallows, biscuits and peanuts to decorate. Put the tray in the freezer for 10 minutes to firm up the mixture.

5. Cut the rocky road into squares and serve.

IN THE BASKET

Marshmallows: based on a 180g bag

Chocolate fingers: based on a 125g box

Notes

Index

S

Acknowledgements

If you're reading this, you're officially the proud owner of my new cookbook, *Feed Your Family for a Fiver in under 30 Minutes!* I simply can't thank you enough for taking the time to go out and buy it. Times aren't easy out there these days, so I hope this book can save you a few quid off your shopping bill!

I've got to be honest with you, I never thought I'd have the opportunity to publish a cookbook, let alone have the privilege of publishing two, so it's all a bit surreal for me that I'm sitting here writing this.

I want to take this opportunity to say a massive thank you to all my followers and supporters for showing my videos, content and also my first book so much love. You don't understand how much I appreciate your kindness. Without you guys, none of this would have even been possible in the first place.

There's so much work that goes on behind the scenes to bring all of this together. So, a special thank you to Lydia Good, George Atsiaris, Sim Greenaway and the whole HarperCollins team and Emily Sweet, who worked so hard to bring this book to life.

Also, huge thank yous and respect to Tom Regester, Katie Marshall and Max Robinson for their absolute graft to make the photos look as incredible as they do. I often find myself drooling over the pages. Proper naughty-looking food.

Finally, I have to give my kids and partner serious credit. They are the ultimate critics and some of the fussiest eaters I've ever had to cook for, so if they like this food, then I know for sure you're going to love it too.

Thank you all again!
Lots of love,

Mitch